Welfare Services for Women and Children

WELFARE SERVICES FOR WOMEN AND CHILDREN

By

Dr. I. Sobha

Department of Women Studies

Sri S.P. Mahila Visvavidyalayam

Trirupati–517502

(A.P.)

2003

DISCOVERY PUBLISHING HOUSE

NEW DELHI-110002

First Published-2003
Reprinted-2010

ISBN 81-7141-663-2

© Author

Published by
DISCOVERY PUBLISHING HOUSE
4831/24, Ansari Road, Prahlad Street,
Darya Ganj, New Delhi-110002 (India)
Phone: 3279245 • Fax: 91-11-3253475
E-mail:dphtemp@indiatimes.com

Printed at:
Sachin Printers
Delhi

Preface

Andhra Pradesh has high child malnutrition, child death rate and maternal mortality rates. Nutrition survey data indicate that majority of pregnant women are suffering from some health disorder. The diet of the people of Andhra Pradesh is deficient in Vitamin A and Riboflavin which fact is partly responsible for the prevalence of blindness.

The Government of India adopted the National Policy for Children which envisaged that "it shall be the policy of the State to provide adequate services to children, both before and after birth and through the period of growth, to ensure their full physical, mental and social development. The State shall progressively increase the scope of such services so that within a reasonable time all children in the country enjoy optimum conditions for their balanced growth". Accordingly ICDS was launched by Government of India on October 2, 1975.

In this context Dr. Sobha's book on reviewing the "Welfare Services for Women and Children" is very much relevant to the present day situation. The book is an indepth case study of ICDS functioning in Rayalaseema region of Andhra Pradesh. The major findings and policy recommendation of this study are relevant for the effective implementation of the scheme in general. The author has explained elaborately the methodology used and the data analysis is lucid. The book will be highly useful to students of social sciences, especially, Women's Studies, Social Work and also to students specializing in Human Development, Nutrition, Child Development and also NGO's and other functionaries dealing with women and children. I wish the author would bring about many more studies relevant to present day issues of women and children.

Prof. K.A. Parvathy

Acknowledgements

The present study on 'Welfare Services for Women and Children', would not have been completed successfully without the cooperation and support from innumerable sources at various stages in the project. Though it may not be possible to acknowledge every one individually, several persons and organisations deserve special mention.

The foremost organisation which needs to be acknowledged is the University Grants Commission, New Delhi, without their financial assistance the present study could not be carried out and the Department of Women and Child Welfare, Government of Andhra Pradesh who have permitted me to conduct the present study in selected ICDS Projects. The Institution where I work Sri Padmavathi Mahila Visvavidyalayam which has permitted me to carry on the work requires special acknowledgement. Prof K.A. Parvathy,. Head. Department of Women's Studies, has been a source of inspiration and I thank her for the encouragement. Dr. S Srinivasan, Deputy Director, NIRD, Hyderabad and Dr. Vijayalakshmi Ramamohan,, and Mr. V. Ravichandra Babu Research Scholar, Department of Sociology, Sri Venkateswara University, Tirupati need special mention for their help in the initial stages of the project. I would like to thank my husband Prof. M S N Reddy, Department of Sociology, Sri Venkateswara University, Tirupati for his constant encouragement at all stages in my academic activity.

I would be failing in my duty if do not thank the CDPOs, ACDPO, Supervisors, AWWs and the beneficiaries of various services who have been my respondents, because it is their responses which have formed the basis for the final shape of the present study.

Ms. P. Neeraja, Project Fellow who took great pains in conducting the field work and for her services at several stages in the preparation of the report deserves a special mention of her sincerity and perseverance and I thank her for the same.

I thank Mr. P. Karthavarayan of Nithin Karthik Xerox for his tidy work in typing the draft.

(I. Sobha)

Contents

1 Introduction

Social services are vital for development of human resources in the rural community. Since the First Five Year plan, there has been an eloquent acknowledgement of the role of social services in national development. Effective integration of social and economic inputs is essential for acceleration of integrated rural development. Social services are designed to enhance the quality of life of the people and to cater to the special needs of vulnerable sections of the society i.e., the children and women, through organised and sustained development efforts.

Children are the most important asset of a country because they will be tomorrows young men/women and provide the human potential required for a country's development. It is, therefore, imperative that today's children should be healthy both physically and mentally so that tomorrow they turn into energetic and dynamic young men/women with alert mind will be able to contribute to a great extent to the national development.

India has not only the second highest population in the world but it also has the second highest child population. About two-fifth of its population are children up to the age 14, and 17 per cent are children under six years of age, a majority of them are raised in families living in extreme conditions of poverty. Consequently, an important indicators of social development, India still ranks low. Infant mortality rate, one of the crucial indicators of child survival continues to be as high as 74 (1993); 30 per cent new-borns are low birth weight babies, and about two fifth of deaths occur in the age group 0-6 years. Further, we have not been able to adhere to the target of universal primary education and control dropout rate at primary level that continues to be as high as 36.27 per cent (1994-95).

Independence ushered in a new era in the field of child welfare/development. It is marked with events which are a testimony to the commitment we have towards our children. Adequate provisions were made for the care and protection of children in the constitution. In order to meet these obligations welfare services have been provided at the national level as an integral part of the country's development plans. Hence, India is taking greater interest in the welfare of children. The constitution of India has provisions relating to their welfare. During the first four five year plans, a large number of programmes were launched by the government for the welfare of children. These programmes were in the fields of health, food and nutrition, education etc., In spite of all these programmes, children in our country still face many problems. A large number of them die before their first birthday. Poverty among our people further increases the problems of our children, especially in rural, tribal and urban slum areas. Infant mortality is much higher in rural areas.

Various surveys have shown that the incidence of malnutrition among children below six years of age is quite high. Vitamin A deficiency which leads to blindness is also common. Diseases like diarrhoea, dysentery, eye infections, skin diseases, respiratory infections and whooping cough are quite common.

The programmes that were initially launched by the government for the welfare of children, each of them dealt with only one problem at a time. There was no coordination among different programmes, and they did not support each other. As a result, the health and general well-being of children and mothers did not show much improvement. For instance, the programme of supplementary nutrition was not supported by health coverage or immunization. While supplementary nutrition was given to the child, no treatment was given if the child got diarrhoea. The child was not protected against diseases such as tuberculosis, polio, whooping cough, diphtheria or tetanus which could be prevented by immunization. Similarly, a programme for health check-up alone would not improve the conditions of the child, if the child needed additional nutrition and this was not provided.

A high powered committee under the chairmanship of Ganga Sharan Sinha, recommended at that juncture that a comprehensive national policy for child welfare was necessary to take an integrated view of different needs of children and assign priorities. As a result of this, the National policy for children was evolved and adopted in 1974. It describes the country's children as a supremely important asset and that is why the needs of children and our duty towards them are enshrined in our constitution. Article 39 of the constitution has laid down in a nutshell our duties and responsibilities towards our children. Accordingly, the tender age of children should not be abused and childhood and youth should be protected against moral and material abandonment.

The National policy has recognized that physical, mental and social development that takes place in early childhood is crucial for subsequent development, and that services provided in early childhood are very important for the development of the child. It has also been realized that all basic essential services for the proper development of the child viz. nutrition, health and education, should be provided simultaneously to children and mothers and right in their own village or ward.

In pursuance of the National policy for children, the Government of India sanctioned the Integrated Child Development Services (ICDS) scheme, which was introduced on an experimental basis on 2nd October, 1975 on the occasion of Mahatma Gandhi's birth day, by the Union Ministry of Education and Social Welfare. Thirty three experimental projects were started in different parts of the country. Each project aimed at the delivery of a package of services in an integrated manner to pre-school children, expectant and nursing mothers and women in the age group 15-44 years right in their own villages or locations.

ICDS is the most comprehensive scheme of the Government of India for early childhood care and development. It aims at enhancing survival and development of children from the vulnerable sections of society, ICDS is a unique programme, it encompasses the main components of human resources development namely, health nutrition and education.

Since its inception, the programme has generated considerable interest among academicians, planners, administrators, and those responsible for implementing the programme. Consequently, a large number of research studies have been conducted to evaluate and assess the impact of the programme on the beneficiaries.

A review of these research studies indicate that ICDS has had a positive impact on beneficiaries and has the potential of enhancing the child survival rate. Definite improvement has been reported on major indicators of health and nutrition like Infant Mortality Rate (IMR), Nutritional Status, Morbidity Pattern, Immunization coverage and utilization of health services.

The Objectives of ICDS programme are: to

1. improve the nutritional and health status of children in the age group of 0-6 years;
2. lay the foundations for proper physical, psychological and social development of the child;

3. reduce the incidence of mortality, morbidity, malnutrition and school drop-out rate;
4. achieve co-ordination of policy and implementation amongst the various departments to promote child development;
5. enhance the capability of the mother, to look after the normal health and nutritional needs of the child through proper nutrition and health education.

With these specific objectives ICDS programme aims at providing a package of services to the mothers and children. It is a unique programme in which all health and nutrition activities essential for promotion of child health and development are included.

The package of Services consist of

1. Supplementary nutrition
2. Immunisation
3. Health check-up
4. Referral services
5. Health and nutrition education
6. Non-formal pre-school education

Availability of safe drinking water is essential for the proper development of the child and therefore, efforts have been made for the coverage of the rural drinking water supply programme in the ICDS project areas. Though it primarily aimed at the care of children and nursing mothers, efforts are also made to bring other related schemes under ICDS project such as safe drinking water supply, sanitation, the Scheme of Functional Literacy for Adult Women (FLAW) etc. were also integrated with ICDS, as an essential component.

The package of services was intended to reach (a) children below six years of age (b) Expectant and nursing mothers (c) women in the age group of 15-45 years. The delivery of services of the different beneficiary groups is as follows:

Beneficiaries	Services
1. Children less than 3 years	1. Supplementary nutrition 2. Immunization 3. Health check-up 4. Referral services
2. Children between 3 and 6 years of age	1. Supplementary nutrition 2. Immunization 3. Health check-up 4. Referral services 5. Non-formal pre-school education
3. Pregnant and nursing mothers	1. Supplementary nutrition 2. Immunization of pregnant women against Tetanus 3. Health check-up 4. Referral services 5. Health and nutrition education
4. Other women between 15 to 45 years	1. Nutrition and Health education.

As mentioned earlier also, the scheme has become the single largest childhood intervention programme in our country. The scheme provides supplementary nutrition to needy children and to expectant and nursing mothers from low income families for 300 days in a year. The aim is supplement the nutritional intake 300 calories and 8-10 gm. of protein for children, 600 calories and 20 gm of protein for severely malnourished children and 500 calories and 20-25 gm of protein for expectant and nursing mothers.

The ICDS projects are located in rural, urban and tribal areas. The administrative unit for the location of the project is community development block in rural areas, tribal development block in tribal areas and slums in urban areas.

In 1991, the number of sanctioned ICDS projects were 2,594 of which, 1,656, were in rural, 711 in tribal and 227 were in urban areas in the country. According to the VIII plan document, by the end of December 1991 about 129 lakh children below 6 years of age and more than 27 lakh pregnant and nursing mothers were given supplementary nutrition under ICDS. About 67 lakh children of 3-5 years age group were getting pre-school education services.

Implementation of ICDS Programme

ICDS, a centrally sponsored programme, is implemented through the state government with 100 per cent financial assistance from the central government for inputs other than supplementary nutrition. The expenditure of the feeding programme is met by the state government from their own funds under the minimum needs programme. Over the years, there has been substantial increase in the funds allocated for ICDS scheme in the central budget which have increased from 337.6 million in 1983-84 to Rs. 2,435 million in 1991-92. The programme is also assisted by a few International organisations like UNICEF, WFP, CARE, NORAD etc.

Type of Beneficiaries

While selecting the location for a project, preference is given to those areas which are predominantly inhabited by vulnerable and weaker sections of the society i.e., SC, ST and families in absolute poverty, such a target group is likely to be found in economically backward areas, drought prone areas and areas in which nutritional deficiencies are rampant, and development of social services is poor. Accordingly the above criteria further determine the priority consideration for selecting the areas for implementation of ICDS project.

Identification of Beneficiaries

Correct enlisting of beneficiaries is an important responsibility of Anganwadi worker (AWW). This is particularly to cover most needy and vulnerable group belonging to landless agricultural labourers, marginal farmers and families with income not exceeding Rs. 11000/- per annum.

As mentioned earlier also, children in the age group 0-6 years have been included as beneficiaries under the scheme. Since, for a child to be healthy, it is necessary that the mother during pregnancy should also be healthy, hence pregnant women are also covered by the scheme. Nursing mothers, during the period when the child is 0-6 months old, also come under the purview of the scheme. Since the mothers play a key role in the physical, psychological and social development of the child, women in the age group of 15-44 years have also been covered under the scheme and will be given health and nutrition education.

Children below the age group of six years, pregnant women and nursing mothers are the principal beneficiaries. Their distribution in the rural, tribal and urban projects is as follows:

1. In a rural project (a community development block) which is assumed to have a population of 1,00, 000 is about 100 villages, 17 per cent of population i.e, 17,000 are less than 6 years (3 per cent, i.e, 3000 are under 1 year, 6% i.e, 6000 are between 1-3 years and 8 per cent i.e, 8000 are between 3-6 years). The number of women in the age group of 15-44 years is estimated at 20,000. Of this, the number of nursing and expectant mothers is estimated at 7000.

2. In an urban project (one or more wards/slums) the number and distribution of beneficiaries is roughly the same as in rural project.
3. In a tribal project (a tribal development block) with a population of 35,000 17% i.e, 5,950 are less than 6 years (3% i.e, 1050 are less than 1 year, 6% i.e, 2100 are between 1-3 years and 8% i.e, 2800 are between 3-6 years). The number of women in the age group of 15-44 years is estimated at 7000. Of this the number of nursing and expectant mothers is estimated at 2,450. The number of villages in a tribal project is around 50.

Method of Delivery of Services

ICDS services are delivered at a community centre, the Anganwadi (literally, a 'courtyard'). The key staff member at this centre is the Anganwadi worker who is invariably a female. The Anganwadi worker is an honorary worker and is given an honorarium of Rs. 563 per month.

Personnel and Functional Structure

The functionaries of ICDS comprise of Anganwadi worker, Supervisor, ACDPO and CDPO. An Anganwadi is the grass-root level organisation to deliver the package of services to children and mothers at their door step. Anganwadis are managed by an Anganwadi worker, and assisted by a helper.

The ICDS project actually functions at block level and the Child Development Project Officer (CDPO) is an overall incharge of the ICDS project., The scheme lays down that preferably CDPO should be a lady and should be a graduate. She will generally supervise the work of 100 Anganwadi workers in all its entirely and this is quite a heavy task. Hence, she is assisted by about four to five supervisors in running the project. Generally there is one supervisor to look after the work of 20 Anganwadi workers.

Apart from the above field staff, the CDPO's are provided with administrative staff for their office.

For efficient delivery of health services under the scheme the health staff at the Primary Health Centre (PHC) has been strengthened from ICDS funds. This additional health staff is as follows:

1. One Health Worker Female (ANM) remains incharge of 5 Anganwadis;
2. One Health Assistant Female (CHV) remains incharge of 6 health workers (females);
3. One Doctor in each one of the PHC.

At the district level the Collector or the Deputy Commissioner is responsible for co-ordination of the programme. At the state level, the Secretary, Department of Social Welfare or the department concerned with ICDS has the overall responsibility for the direction and implementation of the programme. At the central level, the Women's Welfare Department in the Ministry of Human Resource Development is responsible for direction and implementation of the scheme.

Organisational Structure

Broadly speaking, ICDS programme provides health, nutritional and educational support to the children below six years of age and pregnant and lactating mothers. The programme envisages active co-operation of NGOs, realising the need for commitment and sensitivity, available with NGOs.

The programme is being implemented in 23 district of Andhra Pradesh. The total number of projects functioning in the state are 251, (urban 21, rural 201 and Tribal 29) of which 108 are non-World Bank projects. The total AWCs in the state are 36428.

The district women and child development agency, Chittoor has taken up various welfare activities pertaining to women and children through 13 ICDS projects with, 1714 AWCs. Out of 13 projects 9 are functioning under non-World Bank and one under NGO sector, and the remaining are World Bank projects. The number of projects have been increased to 16, with 2047 AWCs in the year 2000. Out of 16 ICDS projects 9 are functioning under non-World Bank, one being run by an NGO and remaining 6 are World Bank projects. Further 5 more are proposed to be started by the year 2002 under Andhra Pradesh Economic Restructuring Project (APER).

Organisational structure of I C D S

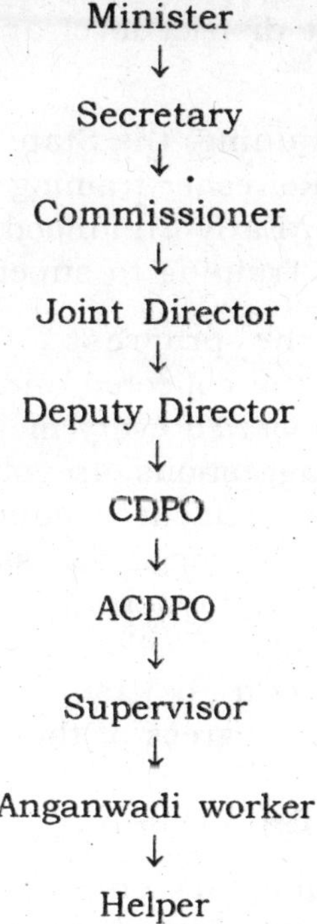

The office of the CDPO consists of the CDPO Sr. Assistant, Jr. Assistant, Typist, Attender, Driver and watchman.

The funds for the ICDS are released by central government through state government. The state ICDS cell will release funds to all projects under various heads as per the requirements. Support is being given by UNICEF for organizing the training programmes and health campaigns.

The scheme is fully financed by Government of India, except the expenditure on supplementary nutrition component which is to be provided by the state government from their own funds.

The expenditure reports should be submitted to the state government by the project officials. Apart from that, auditing will be done by CDPO at project level, Project Officer at district level and Deputy Director at regional level.

Regarding training, the State Government, imparts Job Course and Refresher training to AWWs. Job course, Refresher course, Early Childhood Education (ECE) and Adolescent Girls Training to supervisors and CDPOs.

To record the progress of the ICDS scheme, monthly reports are collected and computerised. These reports will be reviewed every month during the review meetings and suggestions are offered to improve the progress. The department conducts base line survey, end line survey and social assessment on World Bank assisted projects. The external agencies like NIN, ASCI, MODE, MRB etc, conducted evaluation studies and these reports had been utilised to understand the performance and progress of the programme.

Monitoring of ICDS

The programme is characterised by a built-in-monitoring system. The Department of Women and Child Development (DWCD), Ministry of Human Resource Development (HRD) has the overall responsibility to collect and analyse periodic work reports and suggest strategies for timely intervention, thereby ensuring smooth and effective implementation of the programme. The Central Technical Committee (CTC) of the Department monitors and evaluates services related to health and nutrition. It also provides continuous education and training to health functionaries associated with ICDS.

Training

After recruitment and appointment, the functionaries of ICDS programme are deputed by the respective state governments to receive job training in the identified training centres. Further, there is also a provision to impart refresher training to all functionaries from time to time for upgrading their knowledge and skills.

The ICDS programme has evoked considerable response since its inception from students, teachers and researchers due to its multisectoral nature. The scheme has been subjected to intensive evaluation, research and monitoring by Medical Colleges, Home Science Colleges, Schools of social work and other academic and action oriented organizations engaged in child welfare.

2 Review of Literature

A review of various studies that have been conducted on this area is presented under various aspects related to ICDS.

Organisation and Management

Organisational aspects of ICDS implementation were examined by Murthy and Mathur (1986), they pointed out that there is lack of coordination and supervision at the field level, the study found that immunization and health inputs were strong in Gujarat whereas in Uttar Pradesh, the pre-school education and supplementary nutrition received more emphasis as part of ICDS. The evaluation of ICDS by Planning Commission (1982) revealed that the health component did not receive adequate attention unlike pre-school education. In a similar vein, a report from United Nations Population Division says that, a child born in a developing country, is on the average seven times more likely to die before its fifth birthday than a child in an industrialised country. It underlined the need for adequate immunization service, even China reduced its Infant Mortality Rate (IMR), from 266 to 55 during last 30 years (Newstime, 1988). A study in Tamil Nadu (Jaya, 1984) observed that only half of the Anganwadi workers covered health education.

In a study which was conducted in 33 ICDS blocks in West Bengal, it was found that ICDS workers were not sufficiently trained in the use of ordinary teaching aids, hence, visual aids are required for use in the Rural Health Programme. Primary Health Care and ICDS functions were planned, developed and printed under technical guidance and supervision (Johri, NIPCCD, 1989).

After a decade of the working of ICDS, a National conference on Research on ICDS was organised by the National Institute of Public Co-operation and Child Development in February 1986 to take stock of the research conducted on the organisation and functioning of ICDS. The researches have been classified under various heads—Nutrition, Immunization, Health, Health and Nutrition Education (HNE), Early Childhood Development and Education, Community Participation, Impact of Integrated Child Development services, Evaluation of Integrated Child Development services, Monitoring of social components of ICDS and Utilization of services (Research on ICDS: An overview 1975-1985). The researches thus classified show enough evidence to support the fact that Integrated Child Development Service schemes had a positive impact on its beneficiaries and has the potential of enhancing the child survival rate. Research findings also indicate a definite improvement in some of the crucial health and nutrition indicators like Infant Mortality Rate, Nutritional Status, Morbidity Pattern, Immunization Coverage, Utilization of Services etc. The Integrated Child Development Service scheme also has brought about changes in the cognitive development of the pre-school children and the IQ of Integrated Child Development Service scheme beneficiaries was also found to be higher than that of non-beneficiaries.

Nutrition

Adequate nutrition for all is among the most obvious priorities of total development. Malnutrition impairs development and malnourished children are at a greater risk of survival than healthy ones. With the expansion of ICDS projects from 33 in 1975 to 2,594 in 1991, the number of children receiving supplementary nutrition had increased from 1.63 lakhs (October, 1975) to 129 lakhs (December, 1991), and that of expectant and nursing mothers had increased from 4.73 lakhs (March, 1983) to 27 lakhs (December, 1991). Though quantitatively the research conducted on this component of ICDS is quite adequate, still many areas have not been studied. For example, the information related to food and nutrient intake is limited. Prabhakara (1984) and Singhal (1981) found that there was an adequate intake of all the nutrients except Vitamin A in ICDS areas. Joshi (1977) reported that the intake of protein was low. In the study conducted in Tirupati Town revealed that the dietary intake of children revealed a caloric gap of 400-500 and adequate intake of protein. On the other hand few studies reported high incidence of mild and moderate Protein Energy Malnutrition (PEM). About 30 per cent children were suffering from chronic malnutrition resulting in stunted growth (Jyoti Kumari, 1985; Quoted in NIPCCD, 1989).

The fact that the health status of severely malnourished children is poor and incidence of diseases is high among them was corroborated by a study conducted by Tandon (1982). Most of the children suffered with severe malnutrition, had one or more associated illnesses; diarrhoea being the most common one. Udani (1978) also observed that prevalence of illnesses was much more in severely malnourished children. Malnutrition as one of the causes of infant mortality had been reported in the studies conducted by Jugal Kishore (1983), Sunder Lal (1983), Tandon (1983) and Thakur (1984) (Quoted in NIPCCD, 1989).

The prevalence of nutritional deficiencies among children was attributed to prolonged breast feeding with delayed introduction of poor quality supplements (Tarun Kumar, 1983).

The nutritional status of expectant and nursing mothers was assessed in very few studies although it is an accepted fact that the percentage of malnourished women in this group is quite high. In the study by Durge (1979), the values of anthropometric measurements indicated chronic malnutrition among the expectant mothers. It was found that 75 per cent expectant mothers showed signs of nutritional deficiency; 93 per cent were anaemic and had inadequate intake of food rich in minerals and vitamins. Tandon (1978) reported that the distribution of nutritional supplement to expectant and nursing mothers significantly improved. In the study conducted by Gopaldas (1987) efforts were made to formulate a recipe for low-cost, culturally acceptable maternal food supplement for expectant and nursing mothers. Biscuits with 4 per cent fenugreek powder were prepared. Fenugreek imparted bitter taste to the biscuits and hence were unacceptable to children. They were recommended for expectant and nursing mothers because of their therapeutic properties.

In a study by NIPCCD (1990-92) Nutrition services offered under ICDS include supplementary nutrition; nutrition and health education; and prophylaxis against nutritional anaemia and Vitamin A deficiency. Supplementary nutrition is provided to children and to expectant and nursing mothers from low income families for 300 days in a year. The aim is to supplement the daily nutritional intake by 300 calories and 8-10g protein for children; 600 calories and 20g protein for severely malnourished children and 500 calories and 20-25g protein for expectant and nursing mothers. The cost of supplementary nutrition for children, severely malnourished children, and expectant and nursing mothers per day is Rs. 0.75, Rs. 1.25 and Rs. 1.50 respectively. The expenditure towards supplementary nutrition is met by the states under the plan budget available for minimum needs programme.

ICDS scheme has brought significant change in the anthropometric measurements and nutritional status of children and has the potential to enhance it further. Several studies support the claim of positive impact (Sundar Lal, 1977, 1979; Tondon, 1978 (R); 1978 (U); 1987, Bhandari, 1979; 1984; Mehendale, 1982; Patel, 1980; Prasad, 1985; Chandra 1984; Mandowara; CTC, 1990). A few research studies have pointed out that there has been remarkable increase in the percentage of normal children and decrease in the percentage of children suffering from Grade III and IV malnutrition in ICDS areas as compared to children in non-ICDS areas (Mehendale, 1981; 1982; Singhal, 1981; Gupta, 1982; Masood, 1984; Subramaniam, 1984; Thakur, 1984; Chakladar, 1984; Adhish, 1985; Osman, 1987; Barua, 1987; CTC, 1990).

Rajgopal (1985) studied the impact of ICDS on nutrition and health status of children in Madurai (Tamil Nadu). The effect of nutritional supplementation on Grades III and IV Malnutrition was evaluated by a longitudinal study of children over a period of two years. The incidence of the infectious disease was recorded in selected AWC over a period of 5 years before and after complete immunization with triple antigen, oral polio vaccine and measles vaccination. Supplementary nutrition had helped in the improvement of the grades of malnutrition. In 1981, there were 1202 cases of grade III and 232 cases of grade IV malnutrition in the entire block which had been brought down to 862 cases of grade III malnutrition and 153 cases of grade IV malnutrition in 1983. The coverage of immunization was upto 98.5 per cent in 1983 complete absence of whooping cough was reported.

Health Status

The ICDS aims at enhancing the child survival rate by improving the nutritional and health status of children and expectant and nursing mothers through a package of services including health care.

Health component of ICDS comprises health check-up, referral services and immunization. Data available on health indicators suggest that ICDS has potential to enhance the survival rate of children. The package of health services provided under the scheme has certainly improved the health status of children and mothers, which though not upto the optimal level, yet is better than that of children not covered under ICDS. IMR the most important measure of health status of children, has declined in ICDS areas and is also found to be lower as compared to that in non-ICDS areas (Chhikara, 1982; Gupta, 1982; Shah, 1983; Jugal Kishore, 1983; Sunderlal, 1981; 1983; Thakur, 1984; Chandra, 1985; Kushwaha, 1981; Vidya Prakash, 1983; Desai, 1984; Kothari, 1986).

Many children suffered from more than one illness simultaneously or remained sick at one time or the other (Sunder Lal, 1985; Bansal, 1978; Subrahmanyam, 1985). It was observed that 54 per cent of diseases led to loss of weight among infants; the maximum being due to diarrhoea (Swami Saran, 1985).

Sunder Lal (1978) identified 43.4 per cent of children were at risk due to severe Protein Energy Malnutrition (PEM) and 56.6 per cent due to other factors, like more than five siblings in a family, recurrent diarrhoea and respiratory infections, etc.

Nutritionally at risk expectant mothers are likely to deliver low-birth weight babies. Mahapatra (1981) evolved a simplified scoring system to identify expectant mothers at risk and observed a significant direct correlation between high-risk scores and prenatal mortality. Pregnancy and lactation are the periods of physiological stress with an increased requirement for most of the essential nutrients.

According to Visweswara Rao(1969) in poorer socio-economic groups, as the family increases, the food availability per capita decreases. Frequent pregnancies of women substituting on marginally adequate diet impair the health status of women and also impose additional burden of children. Therefore, under existing economic conditions, limitations of family size to three or less children will significantly increase the nutritional status of the fertile women. Superstitions and prejudices seem to prevail mostly among women population especially in rural or urban slum areas. These are known to influence their food intake.

Parvathi Rao (1968) reported that in many regions of Andhra Pradesh, foods of animal origin including milk are forbidden in pregnancy, because of the firm belief that citrus fruits, butter milk, and curds are feared as producing cold, papaya, eggs and black grapes are believed to cause abortions and jaggery to heat up the body system in women. Potatoes, all roots, pumpkin are believed to result in flatulence particularly in pregnant women.

Tondon et al. (1981) conducted a study on evaluation of the delivery system of nutrition and the effect of it on the nutritional status of the children. The study was carried out in 5 rural, 7 tribal and 3 urban project of ICDS. The sample taken for the study was 15572 pre-school children, 940 pregnant women and 3266 nursing mothers. Nutritional anthropometry was used to assess the nutritional status and questionnaire method was used to collect the information. The results reveal that a great number of pregnant women were covered under the antenatal care. The distribution of iron and folic acid tablets and nutritional supplements for the pregnant women was increased in all the three areas. The coverage of lactating women for postnatal care and distribution of supplements was also improved. Nutritional status of the children improved in all the three areas of ICDS project. The impact of ICDS services was most significant among the severely malnourished children. The per cent of these malnourished children was reduced considerably.

Maternal Health Care

The fact that more than 1,00,000 women in India are estimated to die every year from pregnancy-and child birth-related causes, reinforce the importance of ensuring that all pregnant women receive adequate antenatal care during pregnancy and that deliveries taken place under the supervision of trained medical personnel in a hygienic environment.

Antenatal care provides an opportunity for a variety of preventive interventions during pregnancy, including tetanus toxoid injections, and educating women about nutrition, safe delivery, and postpartum care (Govindaswamy et al., 1993).

In a study which was conducted in Tirupati, covering 300 pregnant women, in order to find out the nutritional status of the pregnant women living in the urban slum and utilizing the services of ICDS. A combination of diet survey, anthropometrical, clinical, and bio-chemical methods are used to assess the nutritional status of pregnant women. Through the study it was found that the actual nutrient intake of pregnant women in third trimester for all the nutrients is below the recommended allowance. It was also observed that the diets are deficient in Vitamin C. The intake varies from 26 mg to 43 mg as against 60 mg of recommended allowance (Swarna Latha Devi, 1986).

A study was undertaken by Swarupa (1986) among the pregnant women in the urban ICDS project to assess the nutritional status of the pregnant women and the effect of supplementation on the pregnancy outcome. A sample of 100 pregnant women from 45 Anganwadi centres at Tirupati was selected for the study.

Dietary survey pointed out that the nutrient intake of pregnant mothers especially with respect of calories is only 1700 even after supplementation, leaving still a large gap between the intake and recommended dietary allowances. Even the little supplement of about 460 calories is not completely consumed by the pregnant woman. The reasons for the non-acceptability of the supplement were expressed to be due to its non-conventional form as an extruded product and also because of the bulk of the dry supplement. Cases of grade IV malnutrition in the entire block which had been brought down to 862 cases of grade III malnutrition and 153 cases of grade IV malnutrition in 1983. The coverage of immunization was up to 98.5 per cent in 1983. Complete absence of whooping cough was reported.

HEALTH SERVICES

Utilisation of Services

Utilization of services is another important impact indicator which may be responsible for the difference between an ICDS and a non-ICDS block in the utilization of health services, immunization, antenatal services, deliveries by trained staff and intake of Vitamin A, iron and folic acid tablets (Gupta, 1982).

Information on utilization of health services by expectant and nursing mothers is reported in very few studies. Tandon (1978), Gupta (1982) and Sunder Lal (1979) found that the percentage of expectant and nursing mothers receiving health and nutrition services improved considerably during the repeat surveys. Nearly 70.4 per cent women in an ICDS block and 34.9 per cent and 59.9 per cent in two non-ICDS blocks and 34.9 per cent and 59.9 per cent in two non-ICDS areas were given antenatal care and were immunized against tetanus (Shah, 1983). The utilization of health and nutrition services by expectant mothers was comparatively better in ICDS areas.

Arun Chopdar (1979) evaluated the ICDS programme in Orissa. The study revealed that 80% of the Children and 60% of the expectant mothers had been immunized.

Sixty per cent of the children had received Vitamin A dose, eighty two per cent of the children had received a health check-up and 70% of the expectant mothers had also received antenatal check-up.

The study conducted in 100 ICDS projects from 98 districts in all 25 states and Union Territories. The sample drawn comprised 54 rural, 28 tribal and 18 urban projects. It has revealed that the data on utilization of services for all categories of target population indicated that ICDS programme gave a real boost to the utilization of health services available at the community level. The achievement of health targets laid, in particular for immunization, thus seem formidable with the expansion of ICDS programme.

For all categories of target population studied, it was found that compared to other services in ICDS households, supplementary nutrition was used by a large percentage of beneficiaries. This trend establishes the acceptability of the input by the beneficiaries. It also indicates the potential role ICDS can play in controlling problems like malnutrition, stunted growth, deficiency diseases, low birth weight, complications of pregnancy, etc., so rampant in the vulnerable sections of our society.

Sunderlal (1980) studied the utilization of primary health care services through ICDS scheme in rural areas of Haryana. The pattern of utilization of selected maternal and child health services before and after commissioning of ICDS scheme had been compared. There was a marked reduction of severe degree of malnutrition in the under six age group from 17.6 to 8.4 per cent, which could be attributed to the delivery of package of services and intervention.

Geetha (1989) conducted a study to know the utilization of health services by the community in both ICDS project areas covered by voluntary and government organizations to compare whether there is any difference in the community utilization of health services. The ICDS projects of Tirupati, and Sri Kalahasthi had been selected purposively and studied 400 beneficiary families totally. The findings revealed that the beneficiaries of ICDS run by NGO have better knowledge about the purposes of AWC than the one run by the government. The incidence of common health problems are less among the ICDS beneficiaries run by NGO than among the beneficiaries of ICDS run by government. The Anganwadi workers are also making frequent visits in voluntary ICDS area than those of Government ICDS area.

Immunization

Immunization is an economical and cost effective health intervention of ICDS. PHC and its subordinate health infrastructure carries out immunization of children and expectant mothers. Children are vaccinated against preventable childhood disease like poliomyelitis, deptheria, pertussis, tetanus, tuberculosis and measles, expectant mothers are immunized against tetanus. The immunization status of children in ICDS project areas has improved significantly (Subramanyam, 1985; Santhanakrishna, 1985; Mandowara, 1977). Lack of awareness of Immunization schedule, inconvenient timings, non-acceptance of the vaccine, lack of community participation, superstitions, etc have been identified as the reasons for low immunization coverage (Khanna, 1983; Barua, 1987). It has also been reported that the coverage is generally good for the first dose of vaccine, but the number of beneficiaries decreased for the subsequent doses (Patel, 1980; Modi, 1981). However, the dropout rate has been found to be lower in ICDS areas as compared to non-ICDS areas (NIN, 1990).

In some ICDS blocks information and education regarding immunization was imparted by medical and paramedical personnel but it was not effective. Padmanabhan (1985) observed that private medical practitioners were more effective in advising parents regarding the immunization schedule and the services provided were much better. Incomplete immunization is as good as not being immunized. It has been observed that the immunization coverage is generally quite good for the first dose of vaccines, but gradually for subsequent doses the number of beneficiaries decreases. Patel (1980) found that almost two-thirds of the children dropped out during the third dose of polio and tripple antigen because of febrile reactions following the injection (Quoted in NIPCCD, 1989).

Nutrition and Health Education

NHE component of ICDS aims at enhancing knowledge and awareness of the target women to handle the problems like ill health, malnutrition, diseases etc. which are so rampant in disadvantaged families. The contents of NHE comprise basic health and nutrition messages, effective communication of which can go a long way in improving the well being of children and family.

There are no specific guidelines on frequency of conducting NHE. In the present study around 78 per cent AWWs reported to have conducted formal NHE sessions atleast once in the last three months. The content focussed mainly on messages related to immunization, nutrition, health and hygiene, ORT and breast feeding in descending order of frequency.

It was observed that the mothers who had received health and nutrition education showed significant improvement in their knowledge, attitude and practices regarding infant feeding, deficiency diseases and hygiene and sanitation as compared to mothers who had not received health and nutrition education. The health and nutrition practices in a community were affected by level of education, income and types of occupation of the respondents. In an urban ICDS block, use of Oral Rehydration Services (ORS) and management of diarrhoea was influenced by literacy rate and traditional beliefs and taboos prevalent in society (Rajagopal, 1985).

Health education was imparted to mothers mainly by doctors, neighbours and primary health workers. It was found that the messages given by private practitioners were more effective (Rajagopal, 1985). It was felt that when local leaders were involved in the programme the public was more receptive to health education (Sunder Lal, 1978).

Mushtari Begum and Malathi (1986) conducted a study in Bangalore to determine the nutritional knowledge of mothers who had got educated by the AWWs. Mothers who did not receive any such education on various aspects of nutrition were also evaluated. There were differences between the knowledge levels of the trained and untrained mothers. The mothers who had received training from the AWWs had higher knowledge levels (Komala, 1992).

Supplementary Nutrition

Supplementary nutrition component, is the most popular in the entire package of ICDS programme. The Anganwadi worker was responsible for organising supplementary feeding for children below 6 years of age and pregnant women and nursing mothers at the Anganwadi centre. She was also responsible for planning of menu, for supplementary feeding in consultation with the Child Development Project Officer (CDPO). It was found that the beneficiaries for supplementary feeding were selected very carefully so as to ensure coverage of the most needy and malnourished children. About the benefit received by the children and mothers through this programme, majority of them (86 per cent in Himachal Pradesh and 94 per cent in West Bengal) expressed that they were benefited by this programme (Srinivasan, 1991).

In the study conducted by NIPCCD, supervisors of the study were asked to elaborate on problems faced in distribution of supplementary food. Around 50 per cent supervisors reported that there are problems like delay in supply, incomplete ingredients, low quality material and less than specified/required quantity. Besides the supply related problems, several other constraints were listed which interfered in delivery of nutrition component. The common problems across projects were non-beneficiaries demanding food, children taking food to their home, poor quality of food items, community's interference and poorly maintained records.

Krishnamurthy et al. (1983) in their assessment have found that 48 per cent of the AWCS studied in 16 ICDS projects are providing RTE foods. Whatever be the type of food, the food supplement distributed at the AWCs are divided into two categories; (i) Ready-To Eat food and (ii) food cooked at the AWC. The ready to-eat (RTE) food is essentially pre-cooked. The RTE food is generally processed at the project or state level and distributed to the Anganwadi Centres (AWCs). A number of processing plants have been set up for the production of RTE food. A variety of RTE foods are being used in the ICDS projects. In the data collected by NIPCCD from 232 projects all over the country in 1984-85, it was found that 39 ICDS projects were distributing RTE foods.

Studies on the acceptability of the food supplement provided in the scheme are very few. Desai et al. (1984) reported that in the management of severe malnutrition, though 85 per cent records indicated that children were getting the supplement, actually children consumed half to 'none' of the supplement due to poor appetite. Mothers did not feed the supplement to their children, as 80 per cent of them had diarrhoea, they feared that the supplementary food may worsen it.

Lata Narayan (1983) has also reported that the RTE supplement provided was not acceptable to the children, especially the severely malnourished ones, who were supposed to take double the amount of food. Bread was being used as the supplement in the project studied. Mandowara (1977), in the study conducted at chhoti sadri ICDS project in Rajasthan, also it was attributed that poor coverage of severely malnourished children through therapeutic feeding, due to the monotony of food provided.

The impact of supplementary nutrition also depends on the type of food, regularity of feeding and the adequacy of the food in terms of the prescribed nutrient content. The relevant literature reveals that 10-48 per cent projects serve ready-to-eat foods and that the supplements fall considerably short of the required energy content providing 150-200 cal per child against 300 cal that have been prescribed (NIPCCD, 1984, unpublished). Non-acceptability, as well as unsuitability of food, specially for under-threes, have also been reported (Lata Narayan, 1983).

Malnutrition has been reported to have declined in ICDS project (Tandon et al., 1981). In comparison to baseline figures of 23.2, 29.3 and 22.7 per cent in rural, tribal and urban projects the figures decreased respectively to 11.9, 6.0 and 7.9 per cents. The prevalence of malnutrition decreased from 11.4 to 7.8 per cent in 1983, according to survey reports of the Central Technical Cell (1983). The mortality due to severe malnutrition was reported to have decreased from 15 to 3 per cent.

The PEO evaluation (1982) and Krishnamurthy et al. (1983) found that the coverage of children and mothers from scheduled castes and tribes was better than that of other groups. This may particularly be attributed to the location of the Anganwadi centres in backward areas. Although these findings are encouraging from the point of view of delivering the services to lower socio-economic segments of population, the criteria used for the selection of children for supplementary feeding is supposed to be on the nutritional status based on weight/age or midarm circumference measurement as laid down and not the socio-economic status of the family.

Santhana Krishna et al. (1985) reported the percentage of malnourished children below 3 years in a project operating for 8 years was lower compared to the one operational for 2 years. Knowledge, attitudes and practices of mothers was better in a project established 8 years back, indicating that with longer exposure to ICDS services the impact has increased.

Alternative delivery mechanisms such as 'Creche', 'take home food', 'multi-point feeding' at the Anganwadi centre need to be explored so that the programme will be very popular among rural community. It is essential to give children locally available food. Therefore, it is suggested that CARE food may be given only 'intermittently' for a change (Srinivasan, 1991).

Referral Services

The aim of referral services is to provide adequate medical care to the beneficiaries depending upon the seriousness of their disease and also to follow up cases that have been treated or given medical attention at appropriate levels.

Referral services provided in ICDS programme have not been surveyed by researchers. In an ICDS block, the major referral services rendered were related to health and antenatal check-up. Children suffering from common diseases were also referred to the hospital as the health personnel at the grass root level lacked adequate knowledge regarding their treatment (Natarajan, 1985).

As is evident, many crucial indicators of health status have been surveyed, but there are hardly any studies that give complete health status of the beneficiaries. There are certain areas like referral services, delivery and cost effectiveness of services rendered. Prevalence of deficiency diseases, incidence of vaccine preventable diseases, etc. are the one which need the attention of the researchers. Further, the health status of expectant and nursing mothers has not been reflected adequately, in the studies which have been conducted.

There is a need to have more qualitative and quantitative data on all the health indicators to assess the impact of the programme and to introduce timely modifications in the delivery of services to enhance child survival rate.

Primary Education

'Catch them young' is the proverb for inculcating the appropriate traits in children as early childhood is the period of rapid growth and development. Therefore, the National Policy on Education has placed high priority on early childhood care and education and has emphasized on its integration into ICDS programme. Pre-school education is imparted to the children in the Anganwadis by Anganwadi workers (AWWs) using non-formal play-way methods of learning. With the expansion of ICDS, the number of children attending pre-school has increased from 74,564 in October 1976 to 67 lakhs in December 1991. To sum up, it can be said that non-formal pre-school education, a crucial component of ICDS has improved the enrolment and scholastic performance of children and has had positive impact on their cognitive and language development. If strengthened, it can help in reaching children from the most vulnerable strata of society and enhance their all round development (Quoted in NIPCCD, 1989).

After the Anganwadi starts functioning, the Anganwadi worker (AWW) is expected to perform several activities. She should take care of the cleanliness of the premises and also the pre-school children, SNF distribution, and pre-school education etc. Pre-school education activities include outdoor playing, and indoor playing.

Renuka Khosla (1986) in her study asked the teachers to list the activities which were organised at the centres. Their responses indicate that the main activity was story telling (71.11%), teaching alphabets and numbers (64.44%) action songs (62.22%) out door games (60%), indoor games (55.55%), drawing, painting and clay modelling (53.33%) sand and water-play (20%).

Community Participation

As women were to perform several tasks, routinely at home. She will have no time to concentrate on other things which are not part of the day to day work. Even, she would never think about her own health due to heavy responsibilities at home and at workplace.

A study made by Agarwal is quoted by Asha Srivastava (NIPCCD) parental participation with special reference to their satisfaction and functioning of AWCs was studied by Agarwal in nine villages of Hissar district. The study revealed that a majority of the parents (70%) were not participating in running the AWCs. The expectation level of most of these mothers from AWWs was high (56.67%) and medium (39.33%). A majority of the mothers were some what satisfied with functioning of the AWCs.

The most significant feature of ICDS is to improve the capabilities of the parents to take care of children and thus involve the community by encouraging self help in improving the quality of life and well being of the child and family. ICDS has been envisaged and conceptualized as a community based programme. It calls for community participation in its process of implementation by utilizing local resources. Its objectives are not limited to mere delivery of services, but emphasize initiation of a process aimed at bringing about social change in the life of the community. This is likely to be reflected in change of attitudes, beliefs and practices.

Despite the built in element of community participation, ICDS, in over one and a half decades of its operation, has not been able to involve the community to the desired level. Most of the studies have indicated that the beneficiaries have low awareness about the scheme its components and possible benefits they can derive from it (NIPCCD, 1988; Ramdev, 1982; Sharma, 1986; Sharama, 1987). The participation of the community has been observed to be marginal or low. Only a few isolated individuals come forward to contribute and encourage the programme. The total involvement of the community, its voluntary organizations and other local groups has not taken place as envisaged in most cases. Though the project staff has received training in soliciting community participation, yet supervisors, and CDPOs, by and large were unable to provide AWWs with the desired support and guidance in involving the community (NIPCCD, 1988). Their skills in mobilizing the community have been found to be inadequate.

The study conducted by NIPCCD during 1990-92 evaluated the extent of community participation; The responses of AWWs indicated that it was mainly women (55%) followed by community leader (47%) and adolescent girls (33%) who offered some help in conducting AWWs activities.

In a study by NIPCCD (1984) the information collected from 42 Anganwadies in Kanjhawada ICDS block showed that there was lack of communication between AWWs and various local organisations. The community was providing only marginal assistance in Anganwadi activities. On the other hand, the AWWs had not made a conscious efforts to establish community contacts.

Prabhavathamma (1988) conducted a study in the Rajampet mandal in Cuddapah district to examine the community participation in ICDS project, Ten AWCS centres of the mandal were selected randomly, and 10 mothers from each Anganwadi were selected on random basis. Totally 100 mothers from 10 AWCs were selected as the sample. It was observed that the participation of the local leaders in the ICDS programme is not satisfactory; 15% of them helped in getting accommodation for Anganwadi. Their contribution to immunization, transport, medicine, fuel, storage facilities and so on is nil. But the attitude of the beneficiary respondents and the local leaders towards ICDS programme is positive and they wanted the programme to be continued.

Functionaries of ICDS

Nancy Nagoori (1997) conducted a study in Tirupati town, consisting of 100 Anganwadi workers to know the knowledge of Anganwadi workers in identification of various disabilities. The study revealed that the Anganwadi workers who are in the age group of above 25 years have higher knowledge (57%) than Anganwadi workers of below 25 years (43%) and the AWWs with above 5 years of work experience possessed high knowledge (64%) than AWWs with below 5 years of experience (36%) in identification of disabilities.

In the study conducted in Coimbatore, Out of 93 AWWs available at the time of study 70, who could attend the training programme were selected for the study. The findings revealed that the training programme offered to the AWWs had remarkably enhanced their awareness of disabilities such as mental retardation, visual impairment, hearing impairment and orthopaedical handicaps (Maria Kamalam and Jaya, 1993).

In a study conducted by Baradha and Jothimani (1994) in 20 AWWs under 4 urban projects situated in Coimbatore, 40 children in the age group of 3½ to 4½ years attending the selected AWCs with equal sex representation and their mothers were chosen as sample to study the impact of ICDS on development aspects. All the mothers from the 4 project areas expressed that sending the children to AWC is essential. Ninety three per cent of them stated that AWC fulfills the needs of the children in early years. Nutrition education imparted in the AWC had a good impact on mothers. 100 per cent of them had better knowledge about immunization for both children and mothers.

The study carried out by Jaya and Siva Jyothi Kondraju (1996) on 50 residents of urban slum areas in Coimbatore district, who are the mothers of AW children revealed that most of the respondents were between the age group of 16-18 years and only 40% were illiterates, belonged to low income group. The respondents displayed a marked increase in their awareness on health practices after education.

A study was conducted in 3 ICDS projects namely Tinsukia ICDS project, North-west Jorhat ICDS project and Gowahati Urban ICDS projects of Assam. Forty five AWCS who have undergone job training in the year 1989-90 were selected for the study. The findings revealed that majority (50%) of the AWWs had high level of knowledge on different components of ICDS. All the AWWs maintained the required registers in their AWWs and the availability of teaching aids in the Anganwadis was found satisfactory. It was also found that 80% AWWs used teaching aids in their daily routine for pre-school children.

To examine the position of the Anganwadi and its main functionary, Choudhary (1987) conducted a study in the Garhi ICDS project of Banswara district, Rajasthan. The study was confined to 34 AWCs and their workers. The physical condition of the 34 AWCs revealed that 27 are in rented houses, 5 in school buildings and 2 in temple premises. The buildings of 23 AWCs are Kutcha while 11 Anganwadies are housed in pukka buildings. Proper place to store food and other things were available in 24 AWCs.

The study was conducted in purposively selected Beri Block of Rohtak district, where the ICDS scheme has been in operation for almost a decade by Rajesh Dahiya and Sharma (1990). The study had been conducted among 101 AWCs to know their psychological and social constraints encountered in their day to day work. One of the major constraint expressed by 49.50%, was difficulty in distribution of supplements among beneficiaries due to lack of awareness among villagers about the programme.

A number of studies have also reported that the poor performance of AWWs can also be attributed to the low honorarium paid to them (Singh, 1984; Bidarakappa; Maggie; Satia; Phillips, 1986; Panda, 1990; Widge, 1986; Goriawalla, 1985; Indira Bai; Bhandari; Rane, 1989; Visvesvaran, 1985; RCSS).

In the study conducted by NIPCCD, around one-fourth CDPOs agreed that many AWCs under their charge were not functioning properly. There was fairly good consensus among CDPOs across different projects in attributing this to different reasons. The reasons for poor functioning of ACWs in descending order based on frequency of CDPO's, responses were lack of motivation and skills of AWWs, low level of literacy of AWWs, lack of supervision, supplies not available on time, inadequate training of AWWs and non-utilization of services.

To avoid stagnation and frustrations among the functionaries, avenues of promotion for both AWWs and supervisors have been created. Matriculate AWWs with ten years of experience and supervisors with adequate experience are being considered for appointment against the posts of supervisors and CDPOs respectively. The delay in recruitment and long period for which these posts remained vacant was found to be a factor hampering smooth implementation of ICDS.

It has been said, by Sharma, Adar (1987) and Bhattacharjee (1985) that effective functioning of an

Anganwadi is dependent on a harmonious balance between various administrative factors, its infrastructure, job responsibilities, job satisfaction, job performance, training of functionaries, etc. Many socio-economic factors like age, marital status, educational background, type and size of family etc. have direct effect on the job performance of ICDS functionaries.

After recruitment and appointment, the functionaries of ICDS programme are deputed by the respective State Governments to receive job training in the identified training centres. The training status of ICDS functionaries selected for the study is significantly large number of AWWs and supervisors had received job training.

At the front line of implementation, the support provided by ANMs to AWWs is vital for effective delivery of health services of ICDS package. On analysing responses of AWWs, it was found that ANMs extended support to them in health check-up (57.6%), immunization (79.9%) and referral services (35%). However, for other aspects like identification of children at risk, growth monitoring and NHE, only a small percentage of workers received assistance. There is a need to promote more interaction between these two grassroot workers. ANM has lot of potential to strengthen health components and ways and means have to be worked out to utilize her competence for better implementation of health input of ICDS.

In an ICDS project in eastern Uttar Pradesh, Ray (1990) observed that due to several factors, the Anganwadi centres were not working properly and co-ordinated efforts had not been made to offer better health services and improve the nutritional status of the children. Ray pointed out that in this project, the CDPO and Anganwadi workers were irregular in their work. Functions related to health were grossly neglected by them. In several villages it was reported that the AWWs were frequently absent and orientation of Anganwadi worker was not proper. In several cases, the Anganwadi centres remained closed due to the non-supply of food. It was also informed that a majority of the parents send their children only for supplementary nutrition.

Payments to AWWs and helpers were very meagre and therefore activities with in the AWCs were not undertaken with proper interest by the AWWs. The AWWs spend half their time in maintaining registers and records thereby affecting the other activities of the centre.

"The Manual on Integrated Management Information System for ICDS (1986) says that the Anganwadi worker is responsible for organising pre-school education for children between 3-6 years of age, organising supplementary nutrition feeding for children under six, pregnant women and nursing mothers, making home visits for education of parents, particularly mothers, eliciting community support and participation in running the programme, assisting the primary health centre staff in the implementation of the health component of ICDS programme, maintaining liaison with other institutions in the village and with other village functionaries and maintaining records on village survey and submitting monthly progress reports. A heavy responsibility rests on the Anganwadi workers in respect of helping women to help themselves; in making timely and judicious decisions. This is especially, when the women are confronted with the problems of choosing one or a few alternatives amongst many owing to limited resources at their disposal.

Gopalan's review on ICDS is worth mentioning. He pointed out that, currently the Anganwadi worker is charged with a number of tasks like maintaining records and audits. The time spent by the Anganwadi worker on a task is not necessarily related to its actual importance, but she has apparently neither the knowledge nor the means to correct this anomaly. In short, what is needed is supportive supervision and guidance to the Anganwadi worker so that she can recognise her priorities and can render maximum help to the community within the span of time and with the resources available to her.

Attitude of the Beneficiaries Towards ICDS Programme

A study was undertaken in Pune urban ICDS block to know the views and responses of the beneficiaries towards ICDS programme. A total of 223 beneficiaries were interviewed individually on a pre-tested questionnaire. In all, 94.6% of women were between the age of 18 and 35 years and 64.6% were illiterates. The per capita income was less than 200 rupees per month among the 90% of women beneficiaries. As many as 21% women showed indifference towards attending meetings called by the Anganwadi worker. More than 50% of women informed that they were sending their children to Anganwadi for pre-school education which they felt was definitely useful for the mental development of children and almost all children liked attending Anganwadis.

A total of 34.5% of women did not have correct information about immunization programmes arranged at Anganwadis but majority of women availed the facility of immunization. Most of the women informed that their children were being weighed regularly (monthly). Availability of prenatal services were satisfactory. Beneficiary women noted that supplementary nutrition was regularly available at Balwadis. However, 31.2% of mothers informed that they distributed the SNF items to other children in the family and 56.8% told that they gave less diet to those children receiving supplementary nutrition at Anganwadi centre. Majority of women informed that they have sent their children to Anganwadies for Vitamin A supplementation which was received regularly. Thus in view of the beneficiary women in ICDS, the project was functioning satisfactorily. However, it seems that more emphasis needs to be given on family planning and supplementary nutrition.

Several research studies indicated that ICDS has had a positive impact on beneficiaries and has the potential of enhancing the child survival rate. Definite improvement has been reported in major indicators of health and nutrition like IMR, nutritional status, morbidity pattern, immunization coverage and utilization of health services.

According to the findings of the study conducted by NIPCCD during 1990-92, a large number of rural and urban AWCs were found to have a separate storage place available. It is felt that this provision needs to be made in all AWCs to give the desired face-lift and enough place for organising different activities.

A detailed survey was carried out in a selected ICDS sectors of Madras by Pramila et al. (1986), the sector had 4513 families with a total population of 23,393. Twenty three Anganwadi workers were trained by health educators for creating awareness about ICDS services. The people were made aware of services rendered through ICDS. A Judicious combination of various educational methods were adopted to get active involvement of the people. The information was collected from the people through house visits.

The study revealed that public were not aware of the various services rendered through the Anganwadi centre. The centre was mostly known as nutritious noon meal centre for pre-school children. The investigation further revealed that much effort is needed to motivate the ICDS functionaries to organise methodical nutrition—health education programme to get good co-operation from the public. The public would be definitcly amenable to health education if the local leaders are also involved in this programme. The researcher further recommended that a qualified health educator should be posted in every project to plan, co-ordinate and implement the health education services. The Anganwadi workers needed constant support and guidance to implement health education services.

3 Methodology

In Andhra Pradesh, the Department of Women and Child Development is the nodal department for implementing the ICDS and supplementary nutrition programme. The immunization and health programmes are implemented by the Health Department through Primary Health Centres (PHC). There were 99 ICDS projects (1987) in the State, 61 rural projects, 24 tribal and 14 urban projects and 11,120 Anganwadi centres. Most of the ICDS projects are central projects, of which one has been handed over to the Rayalaseema Seva Samithi (currently Rastriya Seva Samiti), a voluntary organisation in Tirupati. There were 79 projects in the state, at the end of the sixth plan, ten more were added each year in 1985-86 and 1986-87, and 18 new projects have been sanctioned in 1988-89 (Subramanyam, 1990). In 1999, the total number of sanctioned ICDS projects in Andhra Pradesh were 251.

The Government of India with the support of World Bank has planned expansion of the ICDS in four states viz., Andhra Pradesh, Bihar, Madya Pradesh and Orissa. The National Institute of Nutrition, Hyderabad, has carried out studies in the above four states with the following objectives:

1. to establish a baseline key performance indicators;
2. to assess the perception and attitude of the community and functionaries towards the programme; and

3. to understand the strength and weakness in the ongoing programme, so as to suggest a more effective programme in the sample areas.

The results of the preliminary analysis of the data with respect to studies in the State of Andhra Pradesh are presented here:

1. The outreach of all the services that were common to ICDS and non-ICDS areas was relatively better in ICDS areas;
2. The participation of children in the supplementary feeding programme was better (83%) compared to pregnant (68%) and nursing mothers (60%) in the ICDS areas;
3. Overall nutritional status of children (1-5 years) was only marginally better in ICDS areas than in non-ICDS areas. This could be due to the sharing of the supplements with other siblings in the household, as 41% of the children took the supplements home;
4. Physical facilities were inadequate in most of the anganwadis;
5. Anganwadi workers were often constrained by short or irregular supply of supplementary food, drugs, Vitamin A and folifer tablets.

Thus, the study showed that ICDS schemes has improved the outreach of maternal and child health (MCH) and nutrition services, but the maternal component needs greater emphasis. Improvement in the physical facilities and supplies, proper orientation of the functionaries and strengthening of the educational component of the programme are necessary to achieve the objectives of the integrated services (NIN Research Study, 1989-90).

Since, not many sociological studies are available from the state of Andhra Pradesh, the proposed exploratory study examines the organization and management of social services in ICDS programme in sample projects in Rayalaseema region of Andhra Pradesh.

The objectives of the present study are:

1. to study the organisational structure and management of social services with respect to ICDS programme;
2. to assess the health and nutritional status of women and children and to study the extent of utilisation of health services under ICDS;
3. to evaluate the impact of ICDS projects on the health and nutritional status of expectant and nursing mothers and children; and
4. to analyse the perception of the beneficiaries and the extent of their participation in utilisation and implementation of ICDS programme in the sample projects.

Area of Study

The data was collected from both primary and secondary sources. The secondary data was collected from books, journals and various institutional records relating to ICDS projects. In order to collect the primary data through intensive field work, Chittoor district in Rayalaseema region of Andhra Pradesh was selected. This district stands unique with regard to ICDS project implementation, because this is the only district where a non-governmental organisation runs as ICDS project in an urban area apart from non-World Bank aided and Warld Bank aided projects.

Sample of the Study

As a basis for selection of survey areas, a list of the project areas is drawn up in Chittoor district. There are thirteen ICDS projects in Chittoor District. Of these projects, nine are funded by the World Bank, three by non-World Bank agencies and one by a non-governmental organisation RASS (Rashtriya Seva Samithi). One non-World Bank project, one NGO project and three World Bank projects were selected randomly. Within each of these projects ten centres were selected. The criteria for selection of these centres was that, they represent contrasting characteristics such as nearness or farness, economic backwardness or prosperity, educational backwardness or development etc. From within these centres, ten beneficiaries were selected, making a total sample of 500 beneficiaries. The other sample for the study includes the Child Development Project Officer (CDPO), Assistant Child Development Project Officer (ACDPO), The Supervisor (Mukhya Sevika). The Anganwadi Worker (AWW). All the CDPOs(4), ACDPOs(1), Supervisors(23), Anganwadi workers (50) in these centres constitute the sample for the present study. The selection of the beneficiaries was done randomly on the basis of the list of beneficiaries that could be made with the help of the available information with the centres. The sample procedure could thus be described as multistage cluster stratified sampling.

Data Collection

Four different interview schedules were prepared for the four different categories of respondents. The schedules were pretested before they were finalised. Further, observation was also used in addition to asking questions to gather relevant information.

Analysis of Data

The data were scrutinized and verified and was analysed normally as well as with the help of computers. Frequency and percentages were computed for interpretation of the data

Organisation of Data

The report is divided into five parts. The first part consists of introduction and need for the study. The second part consists of review of related literature.

The third part deals with methodological aspects such as objectives, area of study, sample, method of data

Schematic Design of Sample Selection

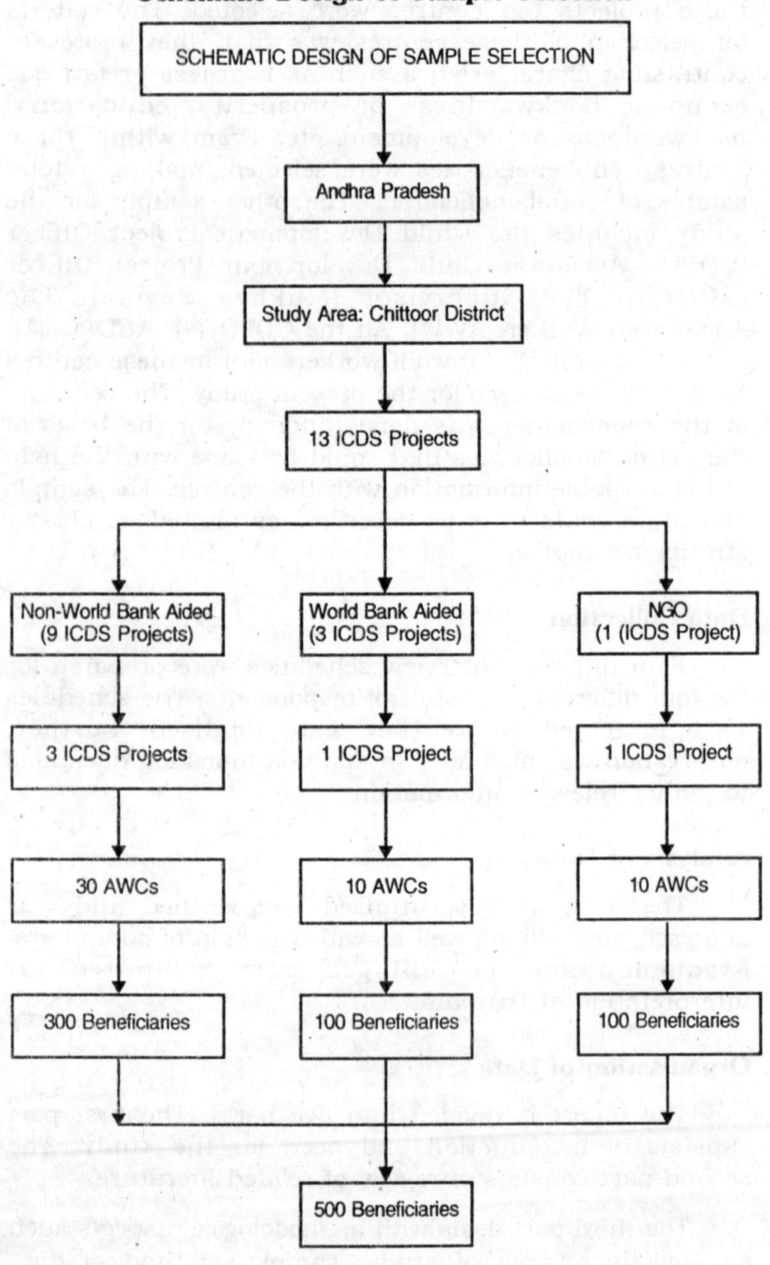

collection, tool for data collection and finally analysis of data.

The fourth part is divided into four subdivisions, i.e.,

1. Beneficiaries under ICDS programme
2. Profile of the Anganwadi workers
3. Profile of the Supervisors (Mukhya sevika)
4. Profile of the ACDPO and CDPOs

Each of these parts is devoted to the results and discussion of the study.

The fifth part presents a summary of the study, conclusions, drawn and suggestions to strengthen the ICDS programme.

4 Results and Discussion

BENEFICIARIES UNDER ICDS PROGRAMME

The study has been conducted in five ICDS projects of Chittoor district, namely Chinnagottigallu (CGL) Srikalahasthi (SKHT), Palamaneru (PLNR) Thamballapalle (TPL) and Tirupati (TPT). Ten Anganwadi centres (AWCs) had been selected from each project. The sample taken for the study was 100 each from Chinnagottigallu, Srikalahasthi, Palamaneru, Tamballapalle and Tirupati ICDS projects, comprising pre-school children, pregnant and lactating mothers, those who were the principal beneficiaries.

Table—4.1 Age of the Children

AGE	CGL	SKHT	PLNR	TPL	TPT	Total	%
1 – 2	4	10	5	18	7	44	17.6
2 – 3	12	12	6	19	15	64	25.6
3 – 4	17	13	12	13	12	67	26.8
4 – 5	17	11	21	–	10	59	23.6
5 – 6	–	4	6	–	6	16	6.4
Total	**50**	**50**	**50**	**50**	**50**	**250**	**100**

The distribution of children according to their age has been presented in Table 4.1. Enquiries revealed that there were no children above four years of age in Thamballapalle project. But in Palamaneru almost all of them were between 3-6 years of age. On the whole almost half of the children were between 2-4 years of age. Among 250 children, ranging between 1 to 6 years nearly 100 children between 1 to 3 years were attending AWC's for Supplementary nutrition food and immunization, rest of the children were availing the above said benefits and also pre-school education.

Table—4.2 Age of the Childrens' Mothers

Age in years	CGL	SKHT	PLNR	TPL	TPT	Total	%
18 – 23	10	21	17	10	15	73	29.2
23 – 28	30	20	20	23	23	116	46.4
28 – 33	10–	3	12	14	38	47	18.8
33 – 38	–	6	1	3	3	13	5.2
38 – 43	–	–	–	–	1	1	0.4
Total	**50**	**50**	**50**	**50**	**50**	**250**	**100**

Among the mothers of children, three-fourths of them were in the age group of 18-28 years. Only 18.8% of them were between 28-33 years of age. Rest of them belong to 33-43 years of age group. Since the respondents were the mothers of children, who were in AWCs this reprcsentation of the age is quite fair.

Table—4.3 Age of the Pregnant Women

Age	CGL	SKHT	PLNR	TPL	TPT	Total	%
<18	2	3	–	–	3	8	5.3
18 – 23	14	18	9	13	14	68	45.3
23 – 28	6	5	15	14	13	53	35.3
28 – 33	6	2	5	3	–	16	10.7
33 – 38	1	2	1	–	–	4	2.7
38 – 43	1	–	–	–	–	1	0.7
Total	**30**	**30**	**30**	**30**	**30**	**150**	**100**

It is also evident from the study that a majority (45.3%) of the pregnant women were between 18-23 years. It is interesting to note that 5.3% of them did not even attain eighteen years of age. This feature appeared in Tirupati, Srikalahasthi and Chinagottigulu projects. It shows that how the parents were quite willing to marry off their daughters at a young age to overcome dowry and social pressures. Further 35.3% of them were between 23-28 years of age followed by 10.75% who were in 28-33 years of age group.

Table—4.4 Age of the Lactating Mothers

Age (in years)	CGL	SKHT	PLNR	TPL	TPT	Total	%
<18	1	1	–	–	1	3	3
18 – 23	8	7	4	10	7	36	36
23 – 28	6	9	8	8	9	40	40
28 – 33	3	2	7	2	3	17	17
33 – 38	2	1	1	–	–	4	4
Total	**20**	**20**	**20**	**20**	**20**	**100**	**100**

The age group of the lactating mothers shows that a majority of (76%) them were between 18-28 years of age. Three per cent of them were below eighteen years, which is an indicator for the existence of the practice of child marriage. Only 4% of them were between 33-38 years of age.

Table—4.5 Religion

Religion	CGL	SKHT	PLNR	TPL	TPT	Total	%
Hindu	77	100	85	49	88	399	79.8
Christian	–	–	5	40	5	50	10.0
Muslim	23	–	10	11	7	51	10.2
Total	**100**	**100**	**100**	**100**	**100**	**500**	**100**

Hinduism being the predominant religion in India, it was not surprising to note that majority of the beneficiaries were Hindus. Only a small per cent (20.2%) of Christians and Muslims were found as beneficiaries in the study.

Table—4.6 Caste

Caste	CGL	SKHT	PLNR	TPL	TPT	Total	%
Farward Caste	44	5	34	48	25	156	31.2
Backward Caste	32	53	29	41	51	206	41.2
Scheduled Caste	22	22	37	11	22	114	22.8
Scheduled Tribe	2	20	–	–	2	24	4.8
Total	**100**	**100**	**100**	**100**	**100**	**500**	**100**

The status and life style of the beneficiaries vary from caste to caste and also within the caste, determined by the traditional occupation, work participation, social interaction patterns and food habits etc. It has been observed from Table 4.6 that about half of the beneficiaries belong to the Backward caste category followed by Forward caste category with 31.2 per cent. Though preference is given to Scheduled caste and Tribes in extending services about one-fourth of the beneficiaries were SC and STs.

With regard to the marital status of the beneficiaries all of them were married but two of them were widows, one in Chinnagottigallu and the other in Tamballapalli project areas.

Table—4.7 Number of Children of the Beneficiaries

No. of children	CGL	SKHT	PLNR	TPL	TPT	Total	%
1–2	75	74	61	72	75	357	71.4
3–4	18	19	32	24	19	112	22.4
5–6	2	1	3	–	1	7	1.0
Nil (1st Pregnancy)	5	6	4	4	5	24	4.8
Total	**100**	**100**	**100**	**100**	**100**	**500**	**100**

Data was also collected about the children of beneficiaries. According to data 71.4% of them had only 1-2 children. 22.4% of the beneficiaries were having 3-4 children. Only 1.4% (7) of the beneficiaries had more than 4 children. 4.8% (24) of the beneficiaries were prospective mothers in their first pregnancy.

Table—4.8 Sex of the Children

Sex	CGL	SKHT	PLNR	TPL	TPT	Total	%
Male	21	32	33	27	26	139	29.8
Female	28	22	19	23	21	113	24.2
Both	42	36	44	45	47	214	46.0
Total	**91**	**90**	**96**	**95**	**94**	**466**	**100**

Of the total 466 beneficiaries, those who were having children, 29.8% of the beneficiaries had male children (Table 4.8) followed by 24.2% who had female children. The remaining 45.9% of them had both male and female children.

Table—4.9 Type of the Family

Type	CGL	SKHT	PLNR	TPL	TPT	Total	%
Joint	19	39	18	26	20	122	24.4
Nuclear	81	61	82	74	80	378	75.6
Total	**100**	**100**	**100**	**100**	**100**	**500**	**100**

It is evident from Table 4.9 that a large number (75.6%) of beneficiaries were in nuclear families. Only 24.4% of them had joint families. It shows that the traditional joint families are fast declining and nuclear families are on the rise even in rural areas.

Details of information related to occupation of the mothers of children, pregnant women and lactating mothers Table 4.10. Diverse occupations were observed among the beneficiaries. According to Table 4.10 more than half of the mothers were housewives. 22.7% of them were leading their lives as labourers. The rest of the beneficiaries engaged themselves by working on their own farm, as food vendors, having petty shops, in weaving and service occupations.

Table—4.10 Occupation of the Beneficiaries

Occupation	CGL	SKHT	PLNR	TPL	TPT	Total	%
Mothers							
Housewives	31	19	26	19	36	131	55.0
Labourer	9	19	12	10	4	54	22.7
Work on their own farm	5	5	–	5	–	15	6.3
Food related business	2	–	–	4	3	9	3.8
Business	2	–	1	–	–	3	1.2
Service	1	4	1	5	7	18	7.6
Weaving	–	8	–	–	–	8	3.4
Total	**50**	**50**	**50**	**50**	**50**	**250**	**100**
Pregnant women							
Housewives	17	17	14	9	20	77	51.3
Labourer	6	10	12	14	1	43	28.7
Work on their own farm	3	2	2	–	–	7	4.7
Food related business	2	–	–	3	3	8	5.3
Business	1	–	1	–	–	2	1.3
Service	1	1	1	4	6	13	8.7
Total	**30**	**30**	**30**	**30**	**30**	**150**	**100**

(Contd...)

Occupation	CGL	SKHT	PLNR	TPL	TPT	Total	%
Lactating mothers							
Housewives	8	8	11	7	17	51	51
Labourer	7	9	9	5	–	30	30
Work on their own farm	1	2	–	3	–	6	6
Food related business	2	–	–	3	2	7	7
Business	1	–	–	–	–	1	1
Service	1	–	–	2	1	4	4
Weaving	–	1	–	–	–	1	1
Total	**20**	**20**	**20**	**20**	**20**	**100**	**100**

Among the pregnant women, 51.3% of them were housewives. More than one fourth of them were continuing their life as labourers. The occupations like agriculture, food related business, business and service etc. were also observed among the remaining beneficiaries.

More than half of the beneficiaries were housewives among lactating mothers. Of the rest who were able to engage themselves in some economic activity, 30% of them were continuing as labourers. The remaining were involved in agriculture, food related business, business, service, weaving etc.

Education serves as a tool to ward off ignorance. It also helps to develop and create awareness about the surroundings and in general, cope with the way of life through acquisition of appropriate skills. It enables the individuals to overcome their prejudices, and wrong notions which prevent the consumption of foods rich in nutrients and breaks the vicious cycle of malnutrition. According to data (Table 4.11) 49.6% of mothers, 45.3% of pregnant women and 44% of lactating mothers were illiterates, followed by 20% of mothers, 22.7% pregnant women and 31% of lactating mothers had primary school education. 28.8% of mothers studied up to 10th class and only 1.6% of them had college education. 30.7% of

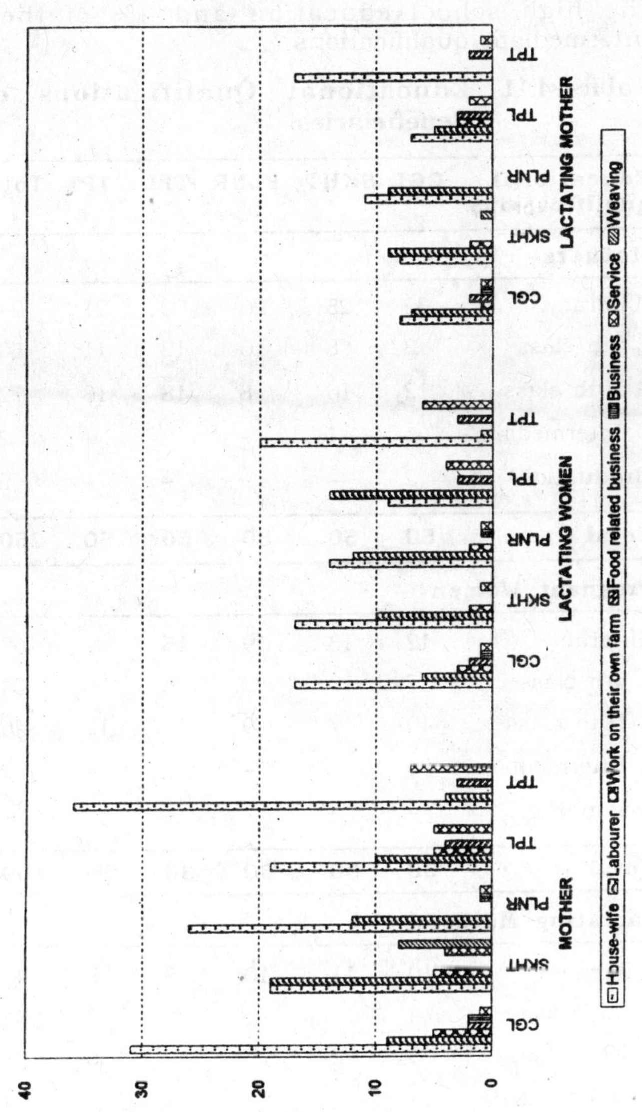

Fig. 4.1: Occupation of the Beneficiaries

pregnant women had high school education but a meagre percentage of 1.3% beneficiaries received the college education. Among the lactating mothers 31% of them had the high school education and 4% of them had intermediate qualifications.

Table—4.11 Educational Qualifications of the Beneficiaries

Educational qualifications	CGL	SKHT	PLNR	TPL	TPT	Total	%
Mothers							
Illiteracy	32	25	26	20	21	124	49.6
£ 5th class	3	8	16	12	11	50	20.0
£ 10th class	12	16	8	18	18	72	28.8
£ Intermediate	1	1	–	–	–	2	0.8
Graduation	2	–	–	–	–	2	0.8
Total	**50**	**50**	**50**	**50**	**50**	**250**	**100**
Pregnant Women							
Illiteracy	12	13	19	15	9	68	45.3
£ 5th class	7	10	2	6	9	34	22.7
£ 10th class	10	7	9	8	12	46	30.7
£ Intermediate	1	–	–	1	–	2	1.3
Graduation	–	–	–	–	–	–	–
Total	**30**	**30**	**30**	**30**	**30**	**150**	**100**
Lactating Mothers							
Illiteracy	10	11	10	8	5	44	44
£ 5th class	4	6	5	8	8	31	31
£ 10th class	6	2	5	3	5	21	21
£ Intermediate	–	1	–	1	2	4	4
Total	**20**	**20**	**20**	**20**	**20**	**100**	**100**

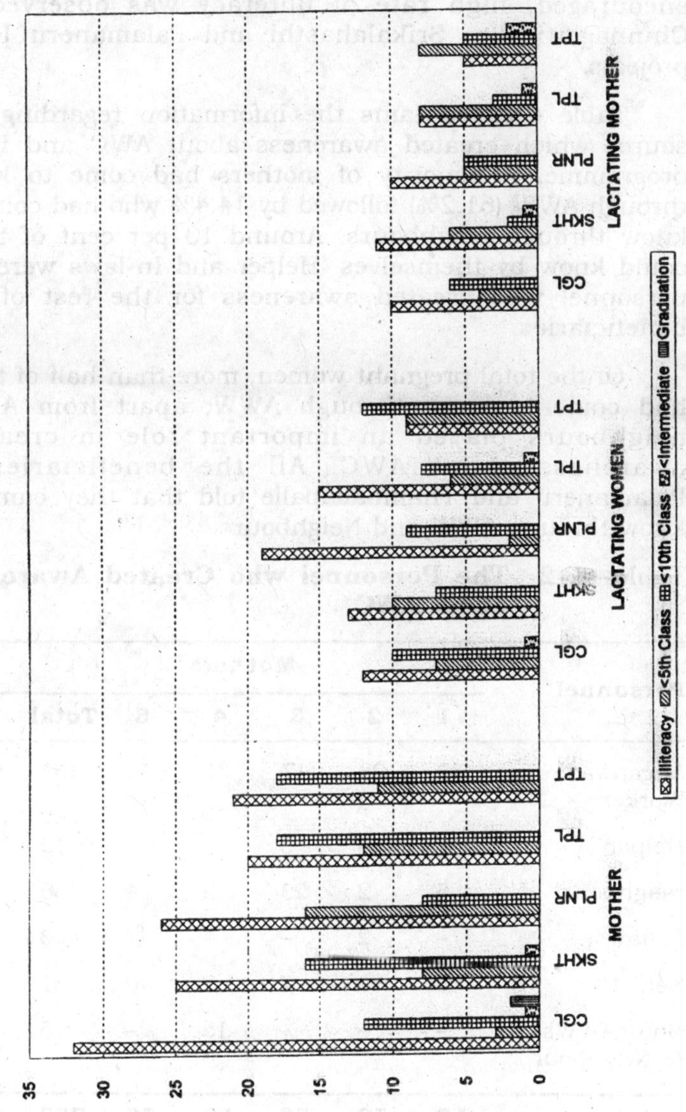

Fig. 4.2: Educational Qualifications of the Beneficiaries

As illiteracy is quite common among rural people where the educational facilities are not in the reach of all the people and education for a girl is not yet encouraged, high rate of illiteracy was observed in Chinnagottigallu, Srikalahasthi and Palamaneru ICDS projects.

Table 4.12 contains the information regarding the source which created awareness about AWC and ICDS programme. A majority of mothers had come to know through AWW (61.2%) followed by 14.4% who had come to know through neighbours. Around 13 per cent of them could know by themselves. Helper and In-laws were the personnel who created awareness for the rest of the beneficiaries.

Of the total pregnant women, more than half of them had come to know through AWW, apart from AWW, neighbours played an important role in creating awareness about AWC. All the beneficiaries of Palamaneru and Thamballapalle told that they came to know through AWW and Neighbours.

Table—4.12 The Personnel who Created Awareness about AWC

Personnel	Mothers						
	1	2	3	4	5	Total	%
Anganwadi Worker	42	28	17	31	35	153	61.2
Helper	–	9	3	–	–	12	4.8
Neighbour	5	2	23	2	4	36	14.4
In-laws	–	2	–	–	1	3	1.2
Self	3	9	7	2	10	31	12.4
Both AWWs & Neighbour	–	–	–	15	–	15	6.0
Total	**50**	**50**	**50**	**50**	**50**	**250**	**100**

(Contd...)

Personnel	Pregnant Women						
	1	**2**	**3**	**4**	**5**	**Total**	**%**
Aganwadi Worker	21	15	12	20	18	86	57.3
Helper	–	–	–	–	–	–	–
Neighbour	7	6	18	–	4	35	23.3
In-laws	–	3	–	–	–	3	2.0
Self	2	6	–	–	8	16	10.7
Both AWWs & Neighbour	–	–	–	10	–	10	6.7
Total	**30**	**30**	**30**	**30**	**30**	**150**	**100**

Personnel	Lactating Mother						
	1	**2**	**3**	**4**	**5**	**Total**	**%**
Aganwadi Worker	13	11	10	10	11	55	55
Helper	–	3	–	–	–	3	3
Neighbour	5	3	9	–	–	17	17
In-laws	–	1	–	–	3	4	4
Self	2	2	1	2	6	13	13
Both AWWs & Neighbour	–	–	–	8	–	8	8
Total	**20**	**20**	**20**	**20**	**20**	**100**	**100**

1: CGL, 2: SKHT, 3: PLNR, 4: TPL, 5: TPT

AWW created awareness about ICDS programme and AWC for 55% of the lactating mothers, followed by 17% for whom neighbours had created awareness. 13% of the beneficiaries, themselves could know about the AWC as they were also going to AWC during their childhood.

According tò data from Table 4.13, majority of the beneficiaries went after few weeks, to AWC after knowing about it. Highest percentage of beneficiary mothers went to AWC after few weeks and 37.2% of them went to AWC immediately after knowing about the programme. Around 12 per cent of them availed the benefits after few moths and years, when there was a need. 1.6% of them told that they knew about the AWC since their childhood and were going to AWC.

Table—4.13 Time Lag Between Awareness and Visiting of AWC

Frequency of visits	CGL	SKHT	PLNR	TPL	TPT	Total	%
Mothers							
Immediately	6	29	23	21	14	93	37.2
After few weeks	44	8	22	27	21	122	48.8
After few months	–	5	5	2	5	17	6.8
After few years	–	6	–	–	8	14	5.6
From childhood onwards	–	2	–	–	2	4	1.6
Total	**50**	**50**	**50**	**50**	**50**	**250**	**100**
Pregnant Women							
Immediately	7	12	14	11	12	56	37.3
After few weeks	23	5	16	19	13	76	50.7
After few months	–	4	–	–	–	4	2.7
After few years	–	7	–	–	4	11	7.3
From childhood onwards	–	2	–	–	1	3	2.0
Total	**30**	**30**	**30**	**30**	**30**	**150**	**100**

(Contd...)

Frequency of visit	CGL	SKHT	PLNR	TPL	TPT	Total	%
Lactating Mother							
immediately	9	10	8	6	5	38	38
After few weeks	11	6	12	14	12	55	55
After few months	–	1	–	–	1	2	2
After few years	–	1	–	–	2	3	3
From childhood onwards	–	2	–	–	–	2	2
Total	**20**	**20**	**20**	**20**	**20**	**100**	**100**

With regard to the pregnant women 50.7 per cent of them availed the benefits after a few weeks followed by 37.3% those who started going to AWC immediately. Though they could know about the programme, 2.7% and 7.3% of them started going after few months and after few years respectively, and the remaining 2% were going from their childhood.

Among the lactating mothers, 55% of them went to avail the benefits after few weeks and 38% of them went to AWC immediately from the day they could know about the programme. 3% had a need to go after few years. The remaining told that they were going since their childhood.

According to data depicted in Table 4.14, 18.4 per cent of the beneficiaries were attending the programmes conducted by AWC on the National festivals like Independence day, Republic day, Children's day etc. More than three fourths of them were participating in pulse polio programme followed by 67.4 per cent of them who were attending mothers meeting conducted by AWC once in a month. Remaining (26.4%) of them were attending AWC to know about the welfare programme GCP, maternity benefit scheme etc. Based on the data it has been observed that majority of the beneficiaries recognised the importance of immunization.

Table—4.14 Programmes Attended in AWC

Programmes	CGL	SKHT	PLNR	TPL	TPT	Total	%
To discuss about National festivals	15	17	20	18	22	92	18.4
To know about welfare programmes	25	27	30	24	26	132	26.4
To participate in pulse polio programme	80	70	85	75	72	382	76.4
To attend the Mothers meeting	62	68	70	72	65	337	67.4

Table—4.15 Type of Benefits got from AWCs

Benefits	CGL	SKHT	PLNR	TPL	TPT	Total	%
Vaccination	–	4	8	–	1	13	26.0
SNF	1	–	1	–	1	3	0.6
Education & Vaccination	–	–	–	77	1	78	15.6
Vacination & SNF	94	37	54	–	29	214	42.8
Education, Vaccination & SNF	5	59	37	23	68	192	38.4
Total	**100**	**100**	**100**	**100**	**100**	**500**	**100**

When asked to specify the reason why they were going to AWC, 38.4% of them told that they went to AWC to avail the combined benefits of pre-school education, vaccination and supplementary nutrition food (SNF) and 42.8% of them told that they went to AWC to collect SNF, and for Immunization. A negligible per cent of 2.6 and 0.6% told that they went to AWC just to have the benefit of Immunization and to collect the SNF respectively.

Among the beneficiaries 67.4% of them have attended monthly meetings, were as 32.6% did not attend. Based on the data highest percentage (96.8%) of the beneficiaries were getting the combined benefits given by the AWC. The details related to SNF are as follows. From 7th month onwards the child will get 80 gms of SNF (weaning food) daily if the child is in 2nd grade. If the child is under 3rd and 4th grade, they get double the share of food i.e. only 135 grams everyday. If the child is in normal or 1st grade they may not get SNF of even 80 gms daily. When the child entered in pre-school education, all the children will get 80 gms SNF daily, in case the pre-school child is malnourished he/she will get 135 gms daily.

Recommended weight		**Grades**
At birth	- 3kgs	100% -80% – Normal
6th month	- 6kgs	79% -70% – 1st grade
1 year	- 9kgs.	69% -60% – 2nd grade –80grams.
2 years	- 12kgs.	59% -50% – 3rd grade –135grms.
3 years	- 14kgs.	< -50% – 4th grade –135grams.
4 years	- 16kgs.	
5 years	- 18kgs.	
6 years	- 20kgs.	
Ex: 6 years	- 13kgs.	$\frac{100 \text{ X } 13}{20} = 65\%$ – 2nd grade

The Table 4.16 shows the reasons for attending the meeting. Among the beneficiaries who attended, majority of them told that they could learn about the importance of different foodgrains. The remaining told that they had been taught about children's nutrition. Nutritive foods to be taken at the time of pregnancy and lactation period, preparation and utilization of Oral Rehydration Solution (ORS) and the practice of cleanliness etc.

Table—4.16 Reasons for Attending the Meeting

Reasons	CGL	SKHT	PLNR	TPL	TPT	Total	%
To learn about importance of food	72	–	59	60	31	222	65.9
Children's nutrition	11	5	31	7	6	60	17.8
Nutrition during pregnancy/Lactating period	5	4	9	2	13	33	9.8
Preparation/ utilization of ORS	–	16	–	–	3	19	5.6
Cleanliness	–	2	–	–	1	3	0.9
Total	**88**	**27**	**99**	**69**	**54**	**337**	**100**

Table—4.17 Reaosns for not Attending and Meeting

Reasons	CGL	SKHT	PLNR	TPL	TPT	Total	%
Heavy work	8	22	1	26	8	65	39.9
Out of station	2	11	–	5	9	27	16.5
AWW didn't conduct	–	21	–	–	–	21	12.9
AWW didn't call	–	8	–	–	11	19	11.7
Lack of interest	–	6	–	–	3	9	5.5
No one to look after the Children	1	5	–	–	13	19	11.7
Husband/Mother in-Law didn't permit	1	–	–	–	2	3	1.8
Total	**12**	**73**	**1**	**31**	**46**	**163**	**100**

Table 4.17 shows the reasons for not attending the meeting for the last 6 months at the AWC. When asked to specify the reason for not attending, 39.9% of them told that they could not attend the meeting due to heavy work. Particularly in Srikalahasthi project, beneficiaries told that AWW did not conduct the meetings and 11.7% were not called by AWW.. Going to other places, lack of interest, child rearing, family members objections etc. were the reasons for rest of the beneficiaries.

Table—4.18 Time Spent at AWC

Time	CGL	SKHT	PLNR	TPL	TPT	Total	%
Few minutes	1	85	2	25	49	162	32.4
Half an hour	70	15	85	72	41	283	56.6
One hour	29	–	13	3	10	55	11.0
Total	**100**	**100**	**100**	**100**	**100**	**500**	**100**

As women have different roles which they have to perform both at home and at work place, majority of them told that they could spare only little time for AWC. A very negligible percentage (11%) told that they could spend nearly one hour at the Anganwadi centre.

Information was sought on how often the project staff viz Child Development Officer (CDPO), Medical Officer, Supervisor, Lady Health Visitor (LHV/ANM) AWW, Helper and any other were contacting the beneficiaries. The data presented in Table 4.19 revealed that CDPO, Medical Officer, Supervisor have not contacted any beneficiary of Srikalahasthi project. On other projects they met the beneficiaries monthly or occasionally.

Table—4.19 Staff Contact with Bencficiaries

Staff	Daily						
	1	2	3	4	5	Total	%
CDPO	–	–	–	–	–	–	–
Medical Officer	–	–	–	–	–		–
Supervisor	–	–	–	–	–	–	–
ANM	–	–	–	–	–	–	–
AWW Helper	100	30	98	99	51	378	75.6

(Contd...)

Staff	Weekly						
	1	2	3	4	5	Total	%
CDPO	–	–	–	–	–	–	–
Medical Officer	–	–	–	–	–	–	–
Supervisor	6	5	–	–	2	13	2.8
ANM	–	–	–	–	2	2	0.4
AWW Helper	–	41	–	1	35	77	15.4
Staff	**Monthly**						
	1	2	3	4	5	Total	%
CDPO	7	–	–	5	–	12	8.0
Medical Officer	7	–	–	5	59	71	14.2
Supervisor	94	55	100	100	37	386	77.2
ANM	100	92	100	100	71	463	92.6
AWW Helper	–	24	2	–	14	40	8.0
Staff	**Occasionally**						
	1	2	3	4	5	Total	%
CDPO	93	83	100	95	–	371	928
Medical Officer	93	36	100	95	6	330	66.0
Supervisor	–	10	–	–	53	63	12.6
ANM	–	8	–	–	27	35	7.0
AWW Helper	–	5	–	–	–	5	1.0
Staff	**Never**						
	1	2	3	4	5	Total	%
CDPO	–	17	–	–	–	17	4.2
Medical Officer	–	64	–	–	35	99	19.8
Supervisor	–	80	–	–	8	38	7.6
ANM	–	–	–	–	–	–	–
AWW Helper	–	–	–	–	–	–	–

In Tirupati ICDS project, CDPO post was vacant for a long time, Medical Officer is incharge of the project.

1: CGL, 2: SKHT, 3: PLNR, 4: TPL, 5: TPT

Fig. 4.3: Staff Contact with Beneficiary

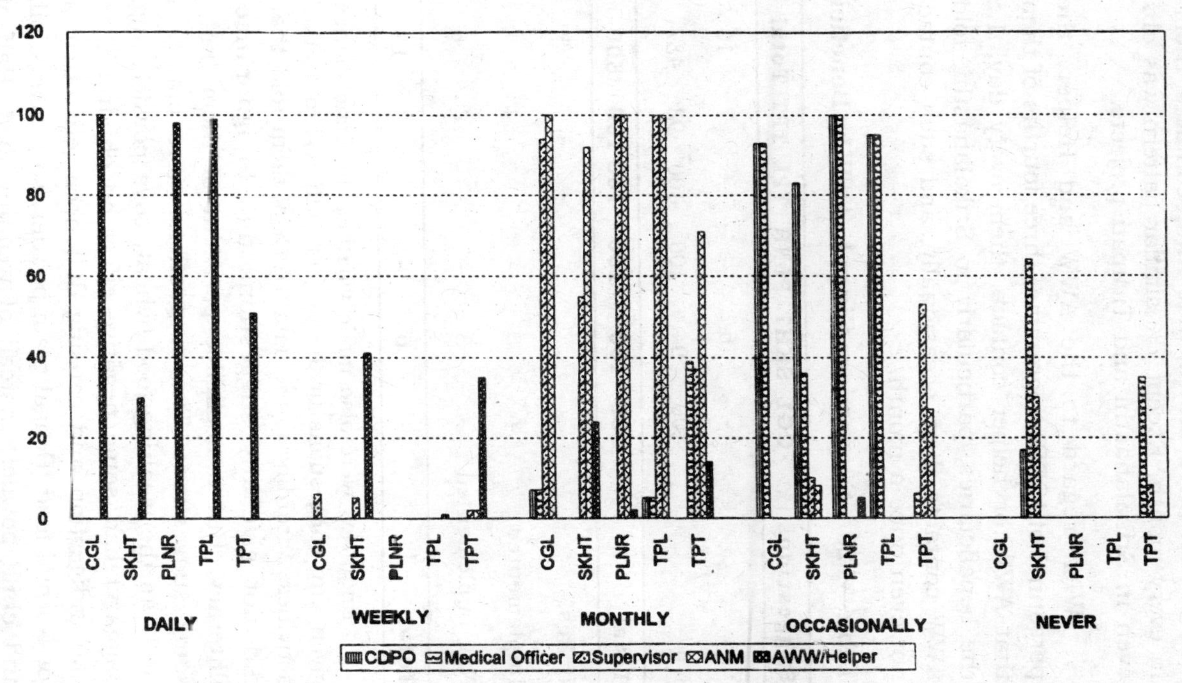

In Chinnagottigallu, Palamaneru and Tamballpalli all the beneficiaries stated that ANM contacts them once in every month. Except 7% similar pattern was observed even in Srikalahasthi and Tirupati projects.

With regard to the AWW and Helper, the key personnel of ICDS programme, three-fourths of them told that AWW or helper contacts them every day. 1.5% of the beneficiaries, particularly in Srikalahasthi, told that AWW contacts them occasionally, and such contact was not even once a month.

Table—4.20 Suggestions Given to AWW by Beneficiaries

Suggestions	CGL	SKHT	PLNR	TPL	TPT	Total	%
Yes	–	6	–	–	7	13	2.6
No	100	94	100	100	93	487	97.4
Total	**100**	**100**	**100**	**100**	**100**	**500**	**100**
If Yes,							
Implemented	–	3	–	–	4	7	53.8
Not Implemented	–	3	–	–	3	6	46.2
Total	**–**	**6**	**–**	**–**	**7**	**13**	**100**

Enquiries were also made whether the beneficiaries have given any suggestions to the project staff regarding the AWW activities. According to the data 97.4% of them told that they did not give any suggestions due to ignorance and illiteracy. But a negligible per cent of them had given some suggestions. The suggestions were mainly about SNF. As the weaning food (wheat, soya powder, sugar or Jaggary) had some negative effect on children's health, like indigestion and causing diarrhoea, etc., they asked for Normal food (Bengal gram powder, soya beans, oil, salt and chilli powder) instead of weaning food. Half of the AWWs implemented their suggestions.

All the beneficiaries were interviewed individually to know their views towards ICDS services, and they have been presented in Table 4.21. The results reveal that except 6.4 per cent of the beneficiaries in Srikalahasthi and Tirupati projects, all the beneficiaries were satisfied with the SNF. Out of 6.4 per cent of them, 2.6 per cent them were not satisfied because of its taste and causing bad effect on children etc.

Table—4.21 Beneficiaries Opinion about ICDS Services

ICDS Services	Satisfied						
	1	2	3	4	5	Total	%
SNF	100	80	100	100	85	468	93.6
Immunization	100	100	100	100	95	495	99.0
Health Check-up Referral Services	60	25	50	70	72	277	55.4
Health and Nutrition Education	80	60	75	86	73	374	74.8
ICDS Services	**Neutral**						
	1	2	3	4	5	Total	%
SNF	–	8	–	–	4	12	2.4
Immunization	–	–	–	–	1	1	0.2
Health Check-up Referral Services	8	–	24	6	8	46	9.2
Health and Nutrition Education	13	–	25	6	8	52	10.4
ICDS Services	**Dis satisfied**						
	1	2	3	4	5	Total	%
SNF	–	5		–	8	13	2.6
Immunization	–	–	–	–	1	1	0.2
Health Check-up Referral Services	–	–	–	–	5	5	1.0
Health and Nutrition Education	–	–	–	–	2	2	0.4

(Contd...)

ICDS Services	No Idea						
	1	2	3	4	5	Total	%
SNF	–	4	–	–	3	7	1.4
Immunization	–	–	–	–	3	3	0.6
Health Check-up Referral Services	32	75	26	24	15	172	34.4
Health and Nutrition Education	7	40	–	8	17	72	14.4

1: CGL, 2: SKHT, 3: PLNR, 4: TPL, 5: TPT

All the beneficiaries, were satisfied with Immunization, in view of the beneficiaries ICDS project was functioning satisfactorily with respect to immunization. 55.4% of them expressed satisfaction on health check-up and referral services, majority of the beneficiaries of Srikalahasthi ICDS projects were not quite happy about health checkup/referral services as the health personnel were not showing much interest on these services. *(See Fig. 4.4).*

The responses given on health and nutrition education show that three-fourths of them were satisfied. 14.4% of them, told that they did not know anything about this service so, they couldn't express their opinion.

Table—4.22 Knowledge about AWWs Educational Qualifications

Knowledge	CGL	SKHT	PLNR	TPL	TPT	Total	%
Aware	70	33	65	60	60	288	57.6
Unaware	30	67	35	40	40	212	42.4
Total	**100**	**100**	**100**	**100**	**100**	**500**	**100**

All the beneficiaries had been asked about their knowledge of the AWW's education, nearly half of the beneficiaries were not aware about their AWW's

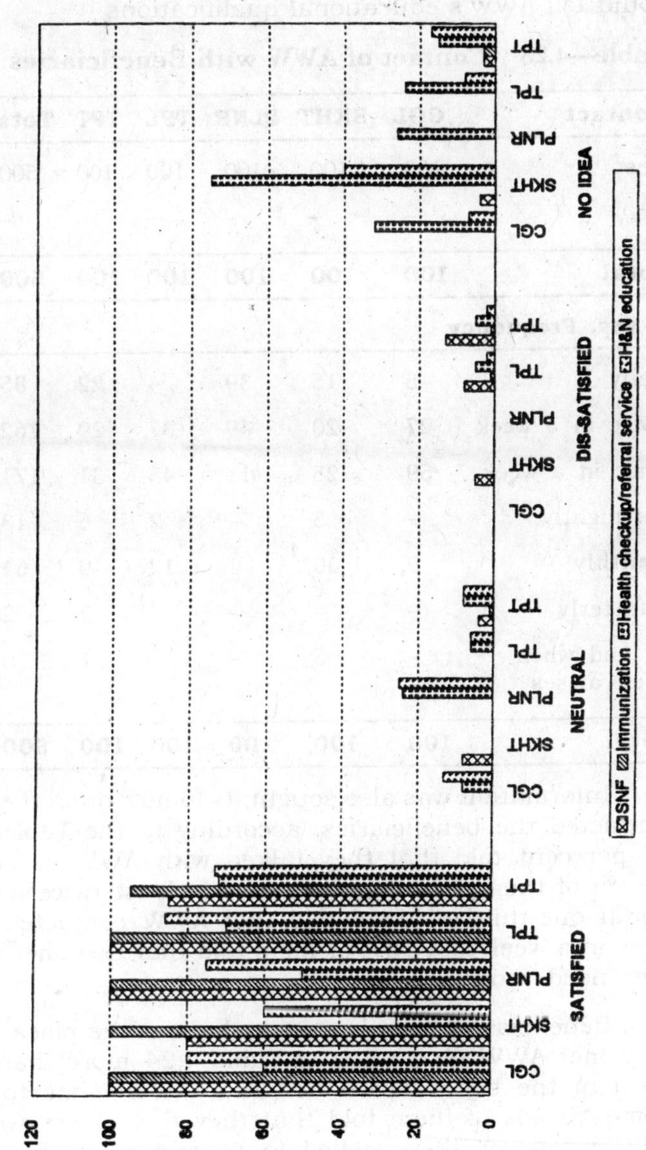

Fig. 4.4: Beneficiaries Opinion about ICDS Services

educational qualifications. The remaining beneficiaries could tell AWW's educational qualifications.

Table—4.23 Contact of AWW with Beneficiaries

Contact	CGL	SKHT	PLNR	TPL	TPT	Total	%
Yes	100	100	100	100	100	500	100
No	–	–	–	–	–	–	
Total	**100**	**100**	**100**	**100**	**100**	**500**	**100**
If yes, Frequency							
Daily	5	15	39	4	22	85	17.0
Twice in a week	27	20	49	37	29	162	32.4
Once in a week	59	25	11	45	31	171	34.2
Fortnightly	–	5	–	2	6	13	2.6
Monthly	9	30	1	12	9	61	12.2
Quarterly	–	–	–	–	2	2	0.4
As and when need arises	–	5	–	–	1	6	1.2
Total	**100**	**100**	**100**	**100**	**100**	**500**	**100**

Information was also sought as to how often the AWW contacted the beneficiaries, according to the Table 4.23, 17 per cent told that they talked with AWW every day. 32.4% of them told that they met at least twice a week. About one-third of them told that AWW contacted them once in a week and 12% of them told that they met whenever need arose.

Beneficiaries have been asked about the place where they met AWW. According to Table 4.24 more than one-third of the beneficiaries told that AWW came to their home. 39.6% of them told that they themselves went to AWC whenever they wished to go and meet the AWW. Around one-fourth of them told that they met either at home or at AWC.

Table—4.24 Place of Meeting

Place	CGL	SKHT	PLNR	TPL	TPT	Total	%
At Home	19	51	61	6	49	186	37.2
At AWC	54	4	38	79	23	198	39.6
Both	27	45	1	15	28	116	23.2
Total	**100**	**100**	**100**	**100**	**100**	**500**	**100**

At the time of collecting data beneficiaries were asked as to when they met their AWW. More than half of the beneficiaries told that they met a week ago., 36.6% said they met 2 days ago, 8% of them informed that they met about a month ago and the remaining (2.6%) did not remember as to when they met because the frequency was very less.

Table—4.25 Nature of Interaction Between AWW and Beneficiaries

Nature of interaction	CGL	SKHT	PLNR	TPL	TPT	Total	%
Enquired about child health	24	18	15	10	14	81	7.4
Given medicines	12	10	14	–	10	46	4.2
Told about nutritive/ weaning foods	30	10	28	–	6	74	6.7
Told about the foods to be taken during pregnancy and lactating period	5	4	3	2	3	17	1.5
Remained about vaccination date	30	16	18	14	10	88	8.0
Told about cleanliness	8	13	12	10	5	48	4.4
Told about Tubectomy	4	9	3	2	3	21	1.9
Enquired about beneficiaries health	–	–	–	–	11	11	1.0

(Contd...)

Nature of interaction	CGL	SKHT	PLNR	TPL	TPT	Total	%
Told about ORS	10	6	4	5	3	28	2.5
Told about the importance of GLV, SNF etc.	100	100	100	100	100	500	45.5
Informed about Maternity Benefit scheme	3	4	3	2	3	15	1.4
Asked reasons for irregular attendance of child	8	4	3	2	4	21	1.9
Called to collect SNF	5	3	1	8	2	19	1.7
Taken the child to AWC	10	8	6	5	3	32	2.9
Informed about GCP	–	3	–	–	–	3	0.3
Told about Immunization and Pre-school education	20	14	16	12	14	76	6.9
Called for meetings	5	4	7	3	1	20	1.8

Enquiries were made about what AWW talked when she met the beneficiaries. According to the data (Table 4.25) revealed nearly half of them told that AWW explained about importance of GLV, SNF, etc. Often AWW discussed about the issues related to health and nutrition of the beneficiaries like how to keep the surroundings, how to prepare ORS etc. and given information about the welfare schemes like Maternity Benefit scheme, Girl Child Protection scheme etc, issues like giving medicines, suggestions regarding the foods to be given to children, weaving foods, foods to be taken during pregnancy and lactation and also explained the importance of Immunization and Pre-school education.

According to Table 4.26 eighty per cent of the beneficiaries extended their help to AWW. The results revealed that half of the beneficiaries were bringing their children to get vaccination. 29% helped in sending the children regularly to AWC, 15% in distributing SNF and the remaining helped in calling the people for meetings. Out of 5 ICDS projects, Srikalahasti and Tirupati projects have extended marginal help to AWW.

Table—4.26 Nature of Help Given to AWW

Nature of help asked	CGL	SKHT	PLNR	TPL	TPT	Total	%
To send the children regularly to AWC	17	31	49	8	35	140	29.1
To bring the children for Immunization	93	6	37	76	36	248	51.6
To distribute SNF	10	13	10	28	11	72	15.0
To help in calling people for meetings	10	–	6	2	3	21	4.3
Total	**130**	**50**	**102**	**114**	**85**	**481**	**100**

When asked to tell their opinion on the overall functioning of AWC, almost all the beneficiaries expressed their satisfaction towards the functioning of AWC, except three beneficiaries from Srikalahasthi who were not happy about the scheme.

Table—4.27 Contact with ANM in the Past Two Months

Number of Times	CGL	SKHT	PLNR	TPL	TPT	Total	%
Once	15	22	65	9	26	137	27.4
Twice	85	78	35	89	74	161	72.2
Thrice	–	–	–	2	–	2	0.4
Total	**100**	**100**	**100**	**100**	**100**	**500**	**100**

According to the data presented in Table 4.27, majority (72.2%) of the beneficiaries met the Auxiliary Nurse Midwife (ANM) once in a month followed by 27.4% who had contacted her once during the past two months and 0.4% of them contacted thrice to get vaccinated or to take medicines etc.

Immunization

Immunization means production of immunity either by introducing vaccine where body system has to take active part to develop antibody or by antiserum when is a readymade antibody. A body needs immunization to be free from the attack of several diseases in future. Hence the provision of immunization services is the other important in built component of ICDS, safeguarding the health of beneficiaries against preventable diseases like Tetanus, Tuberculosis, Poliomyelitis, Diphtheria, Whooping Cough and Measles.

It has been observed that cent per cent of the beneficiaries had knowledge about the vaccination called Tetanus Toxid (TT) which should be taken during pregnancy against Tetanus. They were also aware that this service is rendered at AWC. Data was collected from mothers, pregnant women and lactating mothers to find out their knowledge about vaccination and is presented in Table 4.28.

Majority of mother's of pre-school children told that the pregnant women should be vaccinated during 3-4 months, followed by 14.8% who told that TT should be given during 5th, 7th and 9th months of pregnancy. 2.4% of them could not tell because long back they had this vaccinations, hence they didn't remember.

According to 61.3% of pregnant women, they should get vaccinated during 3-4 months of pregnancy. 14% stated that during 5th, 7th and 9th months, pregnant women has to take TT, but a negligible per cent (0.7%) didn't remember.

Majority of the lactating mothers opined that TT has to be given during 3-4 months followed by 12% who told that 5th, 7th, 9th months were the appropriate time get TT vaccine. According to the data similar pattern has been observed among mothers, pregnant women and lactating mothers.

Table—4.28 Knowledge about Tetanus Vaccine

Months	Mothers						
	1	2	3	4	5	Total	%
1–2	3	–	–	–	–	3	1.2
3–4	47	–	39	43	12	141	56.4
4–5	–	–	–	–	3	3	1.2
5–6	–	–	–	–	–	–	–
3rd & 5th	–	–	8	7	2	17	6.8
5–6	–	–	–	–	4	4	1.6
5th & 7th	–	5	–	–	–	5	2.0
5th & 9th	–	4	–	–	5	9	3.6
7th & 9th	–	–	3	–	3	6	2.4
3rd, 5th & 9th	–	10	–	–	–	10	4.0
3rd, 7th & 9th	–	5	–	–	–	5	2.0
4th, 5th & 6th	–	1	–	–	–	1	0.4
5th, 7th & 9th	–	20	–	–	17	37	17.8
6th, 7th & 8th	–	1	–	–	–	1	0.4
6th, 8th & 9th	–	–	–	–	1	1	0.4
3rd, 5th, 7th & 9th	–	–	–	–	1	1	0.4
No idea	–	4	–	–	2	6	2.4
	50	**50**	**50**	**50**	**50**	**250**	**100**
Months	**Pregnant Women**						
	1	2	3	4	5	Total	%
1–2	1	–	–	–	–	1	0.7
3–4	28	–	24	30	10	92	61.3
4–5	–	–	3	–	1	4	2.7
5–6	–	–	–	–	–	–	–
3rd & 5th	–	–	–	–	–	–	–

(Contd...)

Months	1	2	3	4	5	Total	%
5–6	–	–	–	–	3	3	2.0
5th & 7th	–	13	2	–	–	15	10.0
5th & 9th	–	–	–	–	4	4	2.7
7th & 9th	–	–	1	–	1	2	1.3
3rd, 5th & 9th	–	2	–	–	–	2	1.3
3rd, 7th & 9th	–	3	–	–	1	4	2.7
4th, 5th & 6th	1	–	–	–	–	1	0.7
5th, 7th & 9th	–	12	–	–	9	21	14.0
6th, 7th & 8th	–	–	–	–	–	–	–
6th, 8th & 9th	–	–	–	–	–	–	–
3rd, 5th, 7th & 9th	–	–	–	–	–	–	–
No idea	–	–	–	–	1	1	0.7
	30	**30**	**30**	**30**	**150**	**150**	**100**

Months	Lactating Mother						
	1	**2**	**3**	**4**	**5**	**Total**	**%**
1–2	–	–	–	–	–	–	–
3–4	20	–	14	19	5	58	58
4–5	–	–	3	–	2	5	5
5–6	–	–	3	1	1	5	5
3rd & 5th	–	–	–	–	–	–	–
5–6	–	–	–	–	1	1	1
5th & 7th	–	6	–	–	–	6	6
5th & 9th	–	3	–	–	3	6	6
7th & 9th	–	–	–	–	–	–	–
3rd, 5th & 9th	–	1	–	–	–	1	1
3rd, 7th & 9th	–	1	–	–	1	2	2
4th, 5th & 6th	–	–	–	–	–	–	–
5th, 7th & 9th	–	6	–	–	6	12	12
6th, 7th & 8th	–	1	–	–	–	1	1
6th, 8th & 9th	–	–	–	–	1	1	1
3rd, 5th, 7th & 9th	–	–	–	–	–	–	
No idea	–	2	–	–	–	2	2
	20	**20**	**20**	**20**	**20**	**100**	**100**

However the appropriate time for TT immunization for pregnant women is 16.24 weeks for the first dose 24-32 weeks for the 2nd dose and the maximum interval between doses should be one month, but diverse answers have been given by different beneficiaries. The reason could be that they were not educated properly by AW personnel or the respondents did not evince keen interest.

Table—4.29 The Personnel Who Created Awareness About Immunization

Personnel	CGL	SKHT	PLNR	TPL	TPT	Total	%
Anganwadi Worker	94	56	93	100	64	407	81.4
Private doctor	3	12	–	–	16	31	6.2
ANM	–	22	–	–	4	26	5.2
Elders	–	6	1	–	9	16	3.2
Neighbours	2	–	6	–	1	9	1.8
Govt. doctor	–	2	–	–	3	5	1.0
Self	1	2	–	–	3	6	1.2
Total	**100**	**100**	**100**	**100**	**100**	**500**	**100**

As, it is the responsibility of the AWW to create awareness about the immunization, for more than three fourth of the beneficiaries, AWW was the source to learn about T.T. Private doctor was the source for 6.2%. ANM, Government Doctor, Elders, Neighbours, were the other personnel who created awareness and some of the beneficiaries have come to know by themselves by observing others. All the beneficiaries were immunized against Tetanus during their pregnancy except one beneficiary from Srikalahasthi, which was due to ignorance.

Majority (86%) of the beneficiaries got immunized at AWC (Table 4.30) 7.8% of them went to Primary Health

Centre (PHC), followed by 5% who had immunization both at AWC, for one does and Private Clinic for another dose. The fact that all the beneficiaries got immunized excepting one is a clear indication that they were aware and facilities to get immunized were also available and in the reach of the needy.

Table—4.30 Place of Immunization

Place	CGL	SKHT	PLNR	TPL	TPT	Total	%
In the AWC	80	79	100	96	75	430	86.0
In the PHC	10	10	–	4	15	39	7.8
In the private clinic	10	7	–	–	8	25	5.0
Both in AWC & private clinic	–	4	–	–	2	6	1.2
Total	**100**	**100**	**100**	**100**	**100**	**500**	**100**

According to data (Table 4.31) about three-forth of the beneficiaries got immunized two times during their pregnancy. 17.8% of them got three doses of TT vaccination and 0.2% of the beneficiaries had even four doses of TT. But 8.4% of the beneficiaries told that they had only one dose so far.

Table—4.31 Frequency of Immunization

Details	CGL	SKHT	PLNR	TPL	TPT	Total	%
Once	12	9	2	7	12	42	8.4
Twice	87	30	98	93	60	368	73.6
Thrice	1	61	–	–	27	89	17.8
Four times	–	–	–	–	1	1	0.2
Total	**100**	**100**	**100**	**100**	**100**	**500**	**100**

Table 4.32 contains the information related to the personnel who reminded the beneficiary to get the 2nd dose to TT. As per the data, AWW played and active role in

reminding 68.2% of the beneficiaries, Elders, ANM, Helper, Neighbours were the other members who reminded the remaining beneficiaries. 8.4% of them could remember by themselves. 2.2% of them told that they didn't go for 2nd dose due to fear and the remaining 1.4% told that they had only one dose so far and they will have second dose also when ANM comes to their village.

Table—4.32 The Personnel Who Reminded the 2nd and 3rd Doses

Personnel	CGL	SKHT	PLNR	TPL	TPT	Total	%
Anganwadi worker	67	50	82	82	60	341	68.2
ANM	–	15	–	–	14	29	5.8
Self	14	14	2	1	11	42	8.4
Helper	–	10	–	–	–	10	2.0
Elders in the family	5	4	5		9	24	4.8
Neighbours	–	–	11	–	–	11	2.2
AWW & Neighbours	–	–	–	5	–	6	1.2
AWW & Self	10	–	–	9	–	19	3.8
Yet to go for 2nd time	–	7	–	–	–	7	1.4
Not taken 2nd dose	4	–	–	1	6	11	2.2
Total	**100**	**100**	**100**	**100**	**100**	**100**	**100**

The study revealed (Table 4.33) that 81.6% of the mothers were aware of the various vaccinations like BCG, Polio, DPT and Measles, followed by 9.2% who were also aware about all the vaccines except Measles. 2% of the mothers had no idea about any vaccinations. On the whole, awareness of mothers about different vaccinations was good.

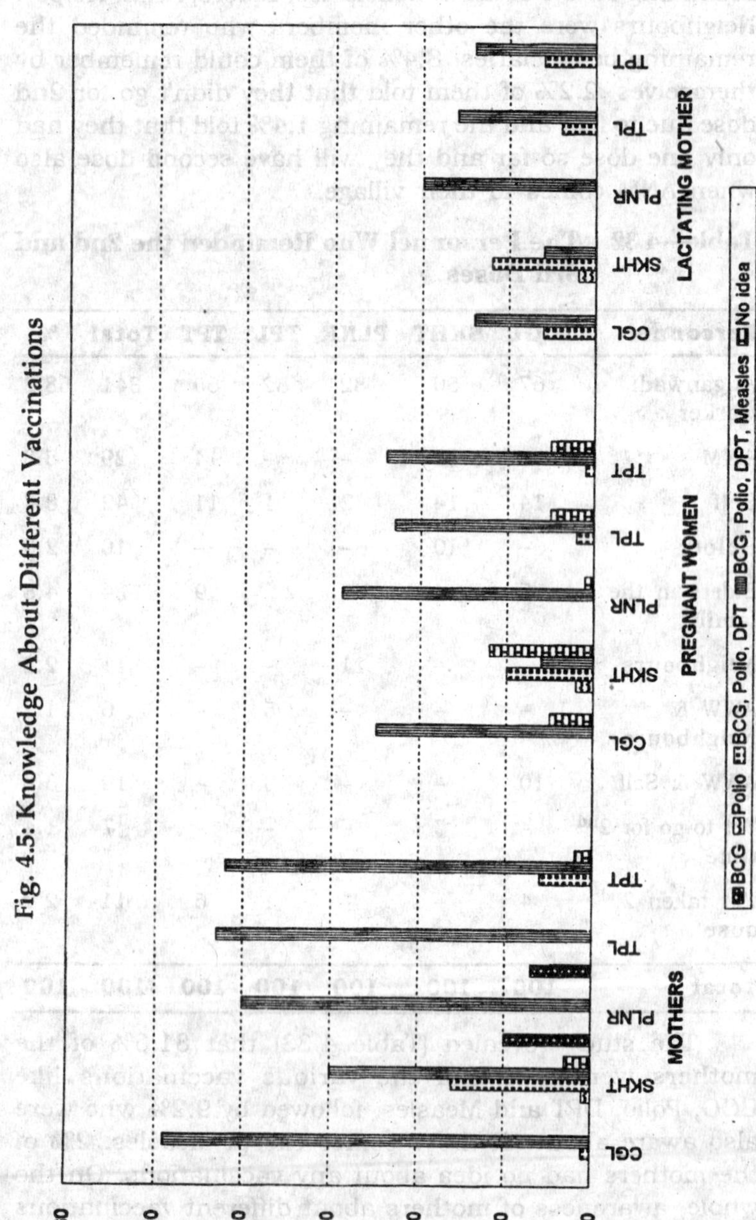

Fig. 4.5: Knowledge About Different Vaccinations

Data in Table 4.33 shows that about three-fourth of pregnant women were aware of BCG, Polio, DPT and Measles vaccinations. 8.7% of pregnant women were unaware only about Measles. If is interesting to note that 18.7% of them were unaware of these vaccines. The reason could be the first pregnancy.

Table—4.33 Knowledge About Different Vaccinations

Type of Vaccinations	Mothers						
	CGL	SKHT	PLNR	TPL	TPT	Total	%
A. BCG	–	–	10	7	–	17	6.8
B. Polio	–	1	–	–	–	1	0.4
C. DPT	–	–	–	–	–	–	–
D. Measles	–	–	–	–	–	–	–
E. a, b, c	1	16	–	–	6	23	9.2
F. a, b, c, d	49	30	40	43	42	204	81.6
G. No idea	–	3	–	–	2	5	2.0
Total	**50**	**50**	**50**	**50**	**50**	**250**	**100**
Type of Vaccinations	**Pregnant Women**						
	CGL	**SKHT**	**PLNR**	**TPL**	**TPT**	**Total**	**%**
A. BCG	–	–	–	–	–	–	–
B. Polio	–	2	–	–	–	2	1.3
C. DPT	–	–	–	–	–	–	–
D. Measles	–	–	–	–	–	–	–
E. a, b, c	–	10	–	2	1	13	8.7
F. a, b, c, d	25	6	29	23	24	107	71.3
G. No idea	5	12	1	5	5	28	18.7
Total	**30**	**30**	**30**	**30**	**30**	**150**	**100**

(Contd...)

Type of Vaccinations	Lactating Mothers						
	CGL	SKHT	PLNR	TPL	TPT	Total	%
A. BCG	–	–	–	–	–	–	–
B. Polio	–	2	–	–	–	2	2
C. DPT	–	–	–	–	–	–	–
D. Measles	–	–	–	–	–	–	–
E. a, b, c	6	12	–	4	6	28	28
F. a, b, c, d	14	6	20	16	14	70	70
G. No idea	–	–	–	–	–	–	–
Total	**20**	**20**	**20**	**20**	**20**	**100**	**100**

Note: A = BCG; B = Polio; C = DPT; D = Measles; E = BCG, Polio, DPT; F = BCG, Polio, DPT, Measles; G = No idea.

Among lactating mothers, all of them were aware of immunization of some kind, 70% of the beneficiaries had the knowledge about BCG, Polio, DPT and Measles 28% of them have known about all the vaccinations except Measles 2% told that they knew only about polio and the importance of polio vaccinations.

Distribution of beneficiaries according to the knowledge about the age when BCG is to be given to children is shown in Table 4.34.

The data reveals that majority of (79.2%) the mothers (beneficiaries) told that BCG is to be given to children at the time of birth. According to 6.8% of the beneficiaries the age is 2-3 months and 8.8% told that 1-2 months. The remaining (5.2%) were unaware about the age.

Most of the pregnant women were not aware of, when BCG is to be given to children compared to mothers of pre-school children and lactating mothers. 60.7% of the pregnant women stated that BCG should be given at the time of birth. BCG can be given in between 1-2 months according to 8.6% of them, in view of the other beneficiaries BCG can be given even between 2 to 9 months.

Table—4.34 Knowledge About the Age When BCG is to be Given

Age	Mothers						
	CGL	SKHT	PLNR	TPL	TPT	Total	%
At Birth	48	32	35	43	40	198	79.2
1–2 months	2	–	8	7	5	22	8.8
2–3 months	–	10	7	–	–	17	6.8
7–8 months	–	–	–	–	–	–	–
8–9 months	–	–	–	–	–	–	–
No idea	–	8	–	–	5	13	5.2
Total	**50**	**50**	**50**	**50**	**50**	**250**	**100**
Age	**Pregnant Women**						
	CGL	**SKHT**	**PLNR**	**TPL**	**TPT**	**Total**	**%**
At Birth	23	11	16	20	21	91	60.7
1–2 months	2	–	4	5	2	13	8.6
2–3 months	–	4	5	–	–	9	6.0
7–8 months	–	1	–	–	–	1	0.7
8–9 months	–	1	–	–	–	1	0.7
No idea	5	13	5	5	7	35	23.3
Total	**30**	**30**	**30**	**30**	**30**	**150**	**100**
Age	**Lactating Mother**						
	CGL	**SKHT**	**PLNR**	**TPL**	**TPT**	**Total**	**%**
At Brith	16	14	15	20	26	81	81
1–2 months	3	4	4	–	–	11	11
2–3 months	1	2	1	–	–	4	4
7–8 months	–	–	–	–	–	–	–
8–9 months	–	–	–	–	–	–	–
No idea	–	–	–	–	4	4	4
Total	**20**	**20**	**20**	**20**	**30**	**100**	**100**

More than three-fourth of the lactating mothers told that BCG vaccine is to be given at the time of child-birth. 4% of the beneficiaries have no idea and between 1-3 months is the right age according to rest of the beneficiaries knowledge.

Actually the recommended age for BCG is at the time of birth. The above revealed that majority of the beneficiaries knew the correct age at which BCG is to be given to children.

Immunization against tuberculosis, diphtheria, whooping cough, tetanus, measles and polio for all children under one year of age in the ICDS project areas has been envisaged under the ICDS scheme. Hence the data has been collected on the knowledge of beneficiaries about the doses of polio and DPT and presented in Table 4.35.

Table—4.35 Knowledge About Polio and DPT Dosages

Doses	Mothers						
	CGL	SKHT	PLNR	TPL	TPT	Total	%
One	5	–	–	–	–	5	2.0
Two	–	–	20	–	3	23	9.2
Three	45	48	28	45	35	201	80.4
No idea	–	2	2	5	12	21	8.4
Total	**50**	**50**	**50**	**50**	**50**	**250**	**100**

Doses	Pregnant Women						
	CGL	SKHT	PLNR	TPL	TPT	Total	%
One	–	–	1	–	–	1	0.7
Two	–	–	2	–	1	3	2.0
Three	24	18	27	25	23	117	78
No idea	6	12	–	5	6	29	19.3
Total	**30**	**30**	**30**	**30**	**30**	**150**	**100**

(Contd...)

Doses	Lactating Mother						
	CGL	**SKHT**	**PLNR**	**TPL**	**TPT**	**Total**	**%**
One	–	–	–	–	–	–	–
Two	–	–	3	–	2	5	5
Three	20	18	17	19	17	91	91
No idea	–	2	–	1	1	4	4
Total	**20**	**20**	**20**	**20**	**20**	**100**	**100**

More than three-fourth of mothers told that the children should have three doses of Polio and DPT vaccinations. 9.2% told that as two doses and 8.4% were unaware of the Polio and DPT doses.

With regard to the pregnant women 78% of them were aware of three doses. But 19.3% of pregnant women had no idea.

As far as the knowledge about the number of doses, 91% of lactating mothers told that three doses are to be given to children. 5% of them told as two doses and the remaining 4% were not having proper knowledge. As per the above data more than three fourth of the beneficiaries had proper idea about the dosages of DPT and Polio.

According to data presented in Table 4.36, it is found that more than half of the mothers stated that the age when DPT and Polio are to be given is 3 to 4 months, followed by nearly one-fourth of them who stated the age as 1½, 2½, and 3½ months, with the minimum interval between two doses should be one month. But 9.6% of the mothers had no idea.

The responses of pregnant women, regarding the age at which Polio drops and DPT vaccines should be given, 51.3% of them told that DPT vaccine and Polio drops are to be given at the age of 3-4 months. 20% of them stated that 1½, 2½, and 3½ months is the appropriate age when these vaccinations are to be given. Around 10% of them had no knowledge about the age when the children should be vaccinated.

Table—4.36 Knowledge About the Age When Polio and DPT are to be Given

Age in months	Mothers						
	CGL	SKHT	PLNR	TPL	TPT	Total	%
1½, 2½, 3½	10	3	7	15	18	53	21.2
3rd, 4th, 5th	–	–	–	–	8	8	3.2
3–4	39	45	29	28	15	156	62.4
4–5	1	–	5	–	3	9	3.6
5–6	–	–	–	–	–	–	–
6th, 7th, 8th	–	–	–	–	–	–	–
No idea	–	2	9	7	6	24	9.6
Total	**50**	**50**	**50**	**50**	**50**	**250**	**100**
Age in months	**Pregnant Women**						
	CGL	**SKHT**	**PLNR**	**TPL**	**TPT**	**Total**	**%**
1½, 2½, 3½	5	4	–	14	7	30	20.0
3rd, 4th, 5th	–	4	–	10	8	22	14.7
3–4	21	16	24	4	12	77	51.3
4–5	1	–	–	–	–	1	0.7
5–6	–	–	6	–	–	6	4.0
6th, 7th, 8th	–	–	–	–	–	–	–
No idea	3	6	–	2	3	14	9.3
Total	**30**	**30**	**30**	**30**	**30**	**150**	**100**

(Contd...)

Age in months	Lactating Mother						
	CGL	SKHT	PLNR	TPL	TPT	Total	%
1½, 2½, 3½	2	8	–	4	4	18	18
3rd, 4th, 5th	–	–	–	–	–	–	–
3–4	17	10	18	16	14	75	75
4–5	–	–	2	–	–	2	2
5-6	–	–	–	–	–	–	–
6th, 7th, 8th	–	–	–	–	–	–	–
No idea	1	2	–	–	2	5	5
Total	**20**	**20**	**20**	**20**	**20**	**100**	**100**

Of the total lactating mothers, three fourth, told that 3-4 months and according to 18% of the beneficiaries, 1½, 2½ and 3½ months of age is the right age to give DPT and Polio and 5% of them had no idea.

The appropriate age for Polio drops and DPT vaccination for children is 1½, 2½, and 3½ months. But 3 to 4 months age is also considerable. The above data revealed that majority of them have correct knowledge about the age when Polio and DPT vaccinations are to be given to the children.

The recommended age for measles vaccine is 9 to 12 months. According to Table 4.37, 68.8% of mothers told the appropriate age to have the measles viccination. 16.8% were unaware about when the measles vaccine is to be given. Compared to other beneficiaries, lower percentage of pregnant women were aware of the recommended age. 20% of them had no idea about the age when vaccine for measles is to be given. Similar pattern was observed even among lactating mothers. Only 61.1% were aware of the recommended age. The next highest percentage (24%) had no idea of the prescribed age.

Table—4.37 Knowledge About the Age When Measles Vaccine is to be Given

Age in months	Mothers						
	CGL	SKHT	PLNR	TPL	TPT	Total	%
9–10	30	32	33	43	34	172	68.8
10–11	8	–	10		6	24	9.6
11–12	4	5	1		2	12	4.8
No idea	8	13	6	7	8	42	16.8
Total	**50**	**50**	**50**	**50**	**50**	**250**	**100**
Age in months	**Pregnant Women**						
	CGL	**SKHT**	**PLNR**	**TPL**	**TPT**	**Total**	**%**
9–10	23	17	11	10	14	75	50
10–11	1	4	6	4	3	18	12
11–12	2	3	8	9	5	27	18
No idea	4	6	5	7	8	30	20
Total	**30**	**30**	**30**	**30**	**30**	**150**	**100**
Age in months	**Lactating Mother**						
	CGL	**SKHT**	**PLNR**	**TPL**	**TPT**	**Total**	**%**
9–10	11	10	12	15	13	61	61
10–11	4	3	3	1	1	12	12
11–12		1	2			3	3
No idea	5	6	3	4	6	24	24
Total	**20**	**20**	**20**	**20**	**20**	**100**	**100**

Details Pertaining to Children

Children in the age group of 0-6 years have been included as beneficiaries under the ICDS scheme. Since the economic status of children has a direct correlation with their general health and nutritional status, the scheme provides the services like supplementary nutrition, immunization, health check-up, referral services and non-formal pre-school education for their overall development. Since mothers play a key role in the physical, psychological and social development of Child, women in the age group of 15-44 years have also been covered under the scheme and are given health and nutrition education.

Table—4.38 Knowledge About the Vaccinations to be Given During 1½–2 Years

Vaccine	CGL	SKHT	PLNR	TPL	TPT	Total	%
DPT & Polio	40	30	35	33	34	172	68.8
No idea	10	20	15	17	16	78	31.2
Total	**50**	**50**	**50**	**50**	**50**	**250**	**100**

About three-fourth of mothers of pre-school children were aware about which of the vaccines are to be given to children during 1½-2 years of age. But one third of the beneficiaries had no idea. It was found that the health personnel were at concentrating on boosters doses of the vaccines which have to be given at different intervals. *(See Fig. 4.6).*

Table—4.39 Knowledge About the Vaccine to be Given at the Age of 5 Years

Vaccine	CGL	SKHT	PLNR	TPL	TPT	Total	%
DT	17	13	15	18	14	77	30.8
No idea	33	37	35	32	36	173	69.2
Total	**50**	**50**	**50**	**50**	**50**	**250**	**100**

As it has been said, the first booster dose should be given when the child reaches 1½-2 years of age with one dose of triple antigen vaccine, and the second booster

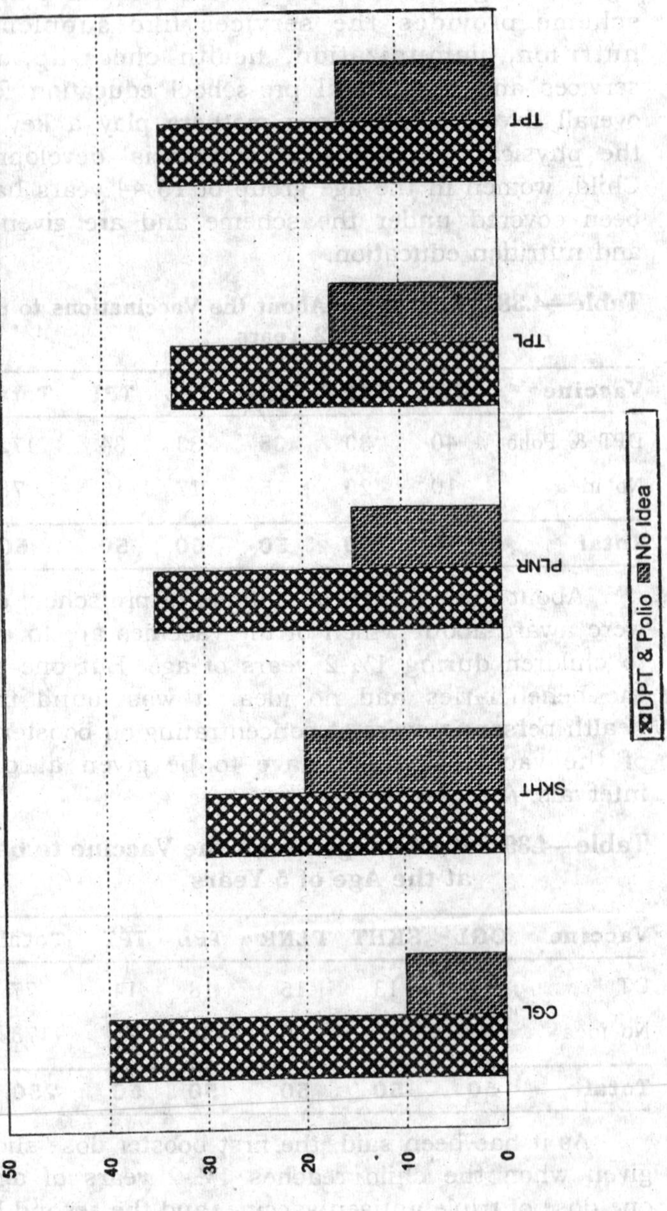

Fig. 4.6: Knowledge About Different Vaccinations to be Given During 1½-2 Years

Fig. 4.7: Knowledge About the Vaccinations to be Given at the Age of 5 Years

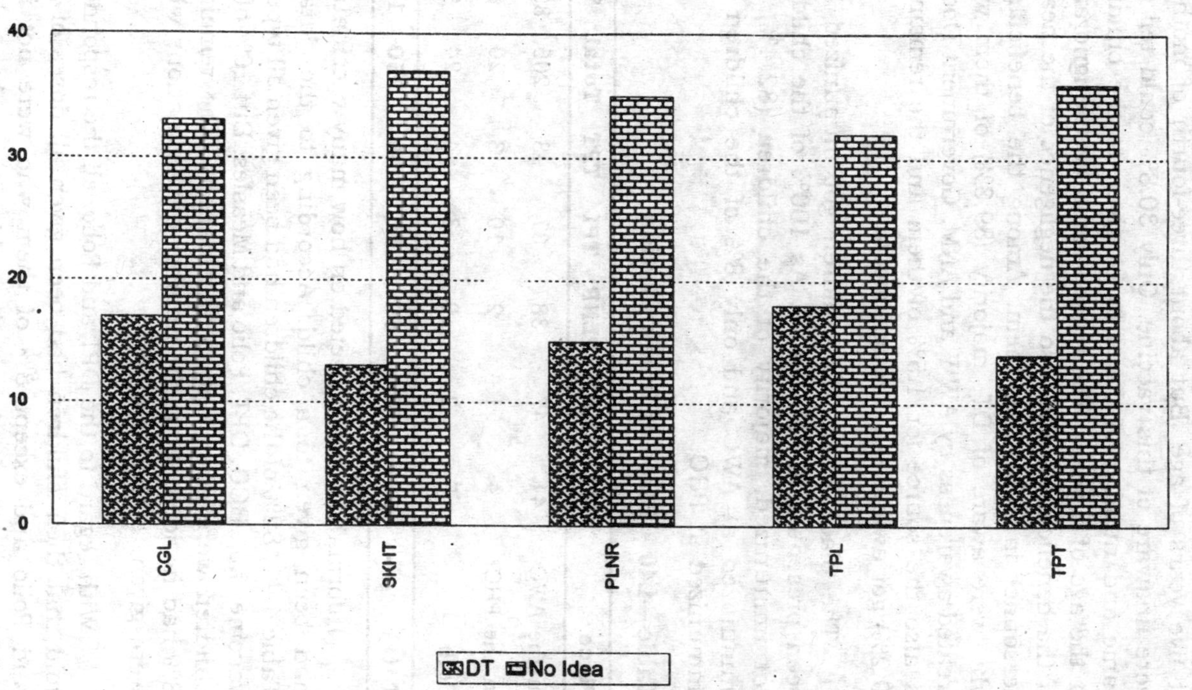

dose with one dose of Diphtheria-Tetanus (DT) vaccine at five years of age. But about three-fourth of mothers were unaware of this vaccine. Only 30.8% could tell the name and number of doses to be given to the children at the age of 5 years. The reason could be the ignorance of the beneficiaries and also the negligence of the health personnel in educating them. Among the beneficiaries who were aware of DT, majority (89.3%) of them were created awareness by AWW and ANM. Government Doctor is also the source for 1.5% of them and the remaining (9.2%) got awareness through media.

The place where the children got immunized has been presented in Table 4.40. As 100% of the children got immunized, majority of the children (82.4%) got immunized at AWC and only 8% of the children got immunized at PHC.

Table—4.40 Place of Immunization

Place	CGL	SKHT	PLNR	TPL	TPT	Total	%
In the AWC	41	47	38	37	43	206	82.4
In the PHC	4	1	2	10	3	20	8.0
Both	5	2	10	3	4	24	9.6
Total	**50**	**50**	**50**	**50**	**50**	**250**	**100**

Information was collected on how many vaccinations had been given to a child. According to the data in Table 4.41, 82% of the children had been given all types of vaccines i.e., BCG, DPT, Polio and Measles. But 10% of the children were given only 3 vaccinations. The remaining 8% had no idea about the number of vaccinations which were given to their children.

With regard to the DPT and Polio, all the respondents told that their children had been given all doses of DPT and Polio and except 8% of them who were not in a position to tell whether their children had these doses or not.

Table—4.41 Number of Vaccinations Given to Children Within One Year

Number	CGL	SKHT	PLNR	TPL	TPT	Total	%
Three	1	10	5	4	5	25	10
Four	41	36	40	43	45	205	82
No idea	8	4	5	3	–	20	8
Total	**50**	**50**	**50**	**50**	**50**	**250**	**100**

Due to ignorance and illiteracy, most of the mothers were least bothered about immunization, hence it was the AWW who reminded nearly 60% of the mothers about further doses of DPT and Polio, followed by Neighbours, ANM, Elders, Helper etc who made the beneficiaries to take all doses of vaccinations (Table 4.42).

Table—4.42 The Personnel who Reminded About Further Doses of DPT and Polio

Personnel	CGL	SKHT	PLNR	TPL	TPT	Total	%
AWW	23	35	28	26	34	146	58.4
ANM	–	6	5	3	3	17	6.8
Elders	–	1	2	–	4	7	2.8
Helper	–	4	3	4	–	11	4.4
Neighbour	–	–	11	–	5	16	6.4
Self	6	4	1	–	4	15	6.0
AWW & Self	21	–	–	17	–	38	15.2
Total	**50**	**50**	**50**	**50**	**50**	**250**	**100**

Majority (96%) of the beneficiaries told that their children had been given BCG. Only 4% had no idea whether their children had BCG vaccine or not (Table 4.43). When asked to specify the age when it had been given, 77.6% of them told that at the birth of their children it has been given. According to 14.4% of the mothers, BCG had been given at the age of 1-2 months, followed by 4% who had been given during 2-3 months of age. The remaining 4% had no idea.

Table—4.43 Details About BCG Given to Child

Details	CGL	SKHT	PLNR	TPL	TPT	Total	%
At birth	47	41	30	43	33	194	77.6
1–2 months	3	4	10	7	12	36	14.4
2–3 months	–	1	6	–	3	10	4.0
No idea	–	4	4	–	2	10	4.0
Total	**50**	**50**	**50**	**50**	**50**	**250**	**100**

Of the total 250 children 84% were given measles vaccine. 13.6% of the children were not vaccinated (Table 4.44) and the remaining (2.4%) mothers had no idea whether their children were immunized or not. Data was also collected about the age as to when it was given and presented in Table 4.45.

Table—4.44 Details About the Measles Given to Child

Details	CGL	SKHT	PLNR	TPL	TPT	Total	%
Given	49	36	40	43	42	210	84.0
Not given	1	13	8	4	8	34	13.6
No idea	–	1	2	3	–	6	2.4
Total	**50**	**50**	**50**	**50**	**50**	**250**	**100**

Table—4.45 Knowledge About the Age When Measles Given to Children

Age	CGL	SKHT	PLNR	TPL	TPT	Total	%
9–10	48	21	27	43	30	169	78.2
10–11	1	4	13	–	2	20	9.3
11–12	–	6	–	–	1	7	3.2
No idea	–	6	2	3	9	20	9.3
Total	**49**	**37**	**42**	**46**	**42**	**216**	**100**

Of the total (216) those who were immunized against measles, all the respondent's children were immunized with in the recommended age i.e. in between 9 to 12 months except 9.3%, who told that they did not have any idea as to when it was given.

Data from Table 4.46 reveals that 77.2% of mothers told that their children had two vaccinations, (DPT & Polio) between 1½ to 2 years of age. But 18.4% of mothers told that their children had not been given any vaccine, and 4.4% of mothers could not tell whether it was given or not.

Table—4.46 Details Regarding DPT and Polio Given to Child During 1½-2 Years

Details	CGL	SKHT	PLNR	TPL	TPT	Total	%
Two	50	25	40	43	35	193	77.2
Nil	-	24	10	-	12	46	18.4
No idea	-	1	-	7	3	11	4.4
Total	**50**	**50**	**50**	**50**	**50**	**250**	**100**

Table—4.47 Reasons for Not Given DPT and Polio

Reasons	CGL	SKHT	PLNR	TPL	TPT	Total	%
Not aware	-	10	4	-	5	19	41.3
AW personnel did not vaccinate	-	4	1	-	2	7	15.2
Under age	-	8	3	-	4	15	32.6
No one remained	-	2	2	-	1	5	10.9
Total	-	**24**	**10**	-	**12**	**46**	**100**

The reason for having not given DPT and Polio vaccines have been presented in Table 4.47. The main reason for not getting immunization was ignorance.

Hence it indicates that AWW did not put serious effort in creating awareness or the respondents did not evince interest. 15.2% of the mothers told that their children were not feeling well at the time of vaccination, hence, AW personnel didn't vaccinate. Relatively higher 32.6% of mothers told that their children had not yet attained the recommended age, so they didn't get vaccinated.

Table—4.48 Personnel Who Remained About Polio and DPT Booster Doses

Personnel	CGL	SKHT	PLNR	TPL	TPT	Total	%
AWW	29	16	25	20	31	121	59.3
Neighbour	–	–	12	16	–	28	13.7
ANM	1	4	–	–	3	8	3.9
Helper	–	5	–	–	–	5	2.5
Self	1	1	3	7	1	13	6.4
AWW & Self	19	–	–	7	3	29	14.2
Total	**50**	**26**	**40**	**50**	**38**	**204**	**100**

AWW played an active role in making them to get vaccination, followed by neighbours, ANM and Helper who helped the beneficiaries by reminding them about booster doses.

Table—4.49 Details About the Booster Dose Given to Child at the Age of 5 Years

Details	CGL	SKHT	PLNR	TPL	TPT	Total	%
Given	6	8	24	16	12	66	26.4
Not given	44	42	26	34	38	184	73.6
Total	**50**	**50**	**50**	**50**	**50**	**250**	**100**

With regard to the booster dose, which is to be given at 5 years of age, three-fourth of the children were not given booster doses. The reasons expressed by the beneficiaries were more than half (57%) of the children were below the age of 5 years were as they could be vaccinated at 5 years of age. 36.3% of mothers were not aware of booster dose. The remaining 6.7%, particularly in Thamballapalle Project, mothers told that their AW personnel didn't vaccinate the children. Of the one-fourth (26.4%), who were immunized, most of them (82%) were reminded by AWW rest of them were reminded through helper and ANM.

Details Pertaining to Pregnant Women

For a child to be healthy it is necessary that the mother during her pregnancy should also be healthy. Hence, pregnant women are also covered by the scheme and are provided the services like supplementary nutrition, immunization against tetanus, health check-up, referral services and health and nutrition education. The aim of supplementary nutrition is to provide the food intake consisting of about 500 calories and 25 grams of protein for pregnant women.

Table—4.50 Month of Pregnancy

Month	CGL	SKHT	PLNR	TPL	TPT	Total	%
3–5	4	4	3	2	6	19	12.7
5–7	13	10	9	15	13	60	40.0
7–9	13	16	18	13	11	71	47.3
Total	**30**	**30**	**30**	**30**	**30**	**150**	**100**

At the time of data collection about half of the beneficiaries were in 7-9 months of pregnancy 40% of them were between 5-7 months followed by 12.7% who were within 3-5 months of pregnancy. Generally pregnant women are enrolled after the completion of 3rd month.

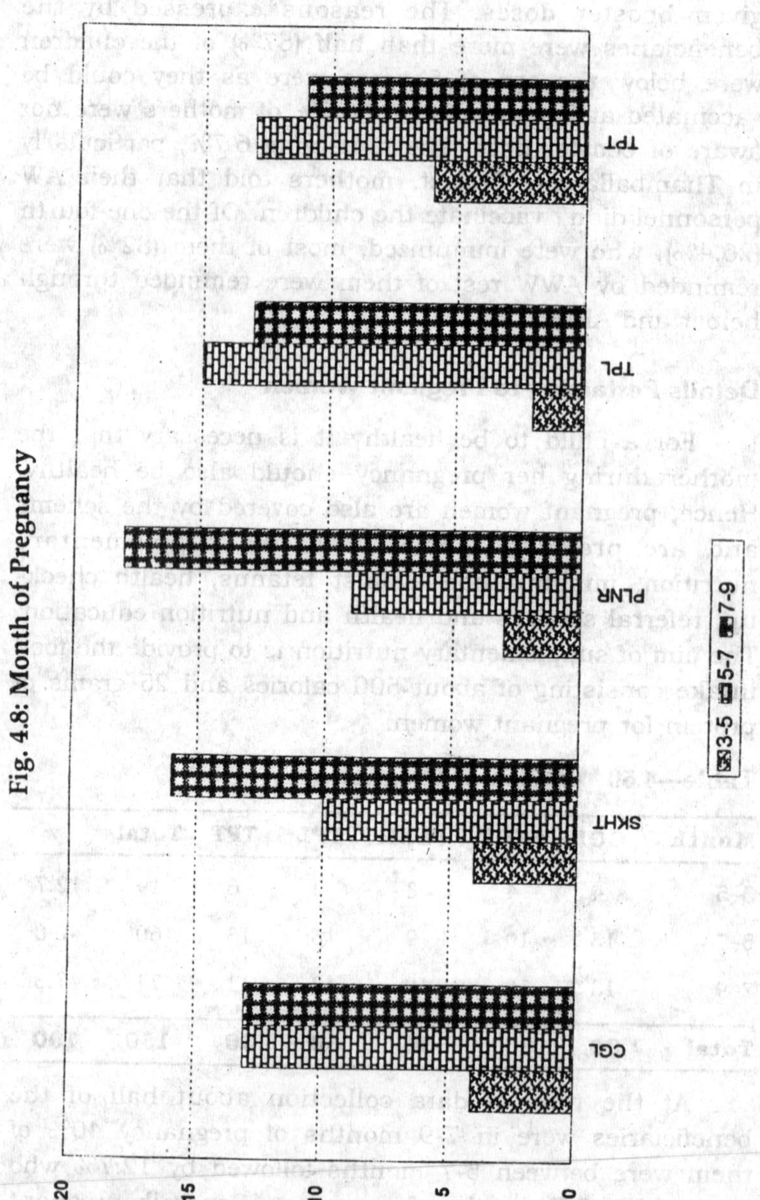

Fig. 4.8: Month of Pregnancy

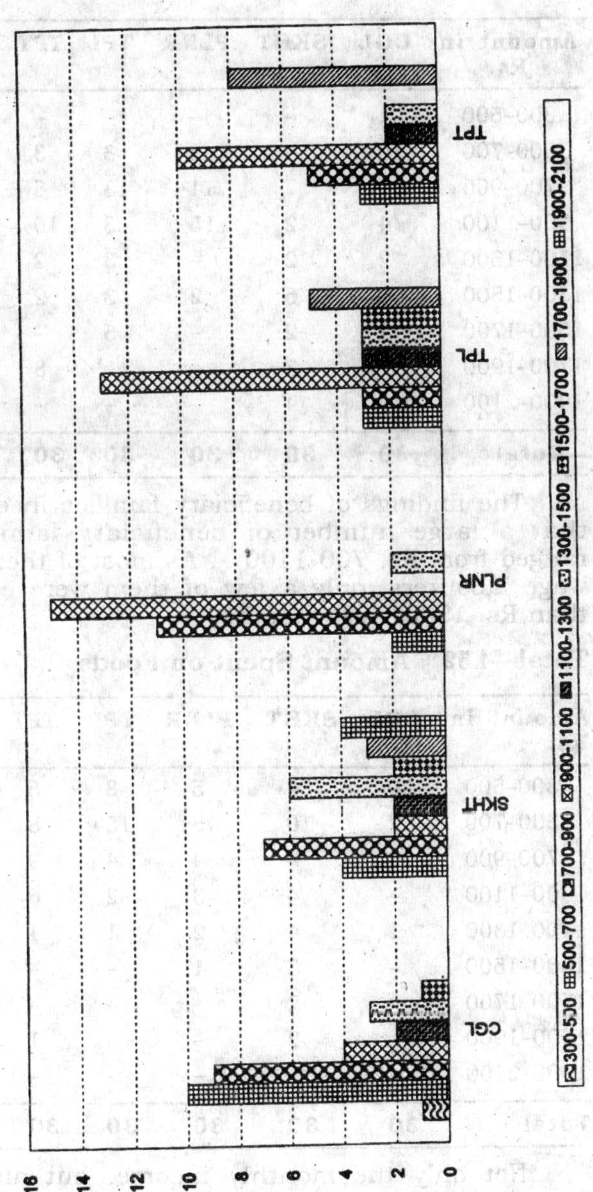

Fig. 4.9: Monthly Income of the Family

Table—4.51 Monthly Income of the Family

Amount in Rs.	CGL	SKHT	PLNR	TPL	TPT	Total	%
300–500	1	–	–	–	–	1	0.6
500–700	10	4	2	3	3	22	14.7
700–900	9	7	11	13	5	45	30.0
900–1100	4	2	15	3	10	34	22.7
1100–1300	2	2	–	3	2	9	6.0
1300–1500	3	6	2	3	2	16	10.7
1500–1700	1	2	–	5	–	8	5.3
1700–1900	–	3	–	–	8	11	7.3
1900–2100	–	4	–	–	–	4	2.7
Total	**30**	**30**	**30**	**30**	**30**	**150**	**100**

The findings of beneficiary families income revealed that a large number of beneficiary families income ranged from Rs. 700-1100/-. As most of them were daily wage labourers, only a few of them were earning more than Rs. 1500/- per month.

Total—4.52 Amount Spent on Foods

Amount in Rs.	CGL	SKHT	PLNR	TPL	TPT	Total	%
300–500	20	4	5	8	5	42	28.0
500–700	7	10	15	15	8	55	36.7
700–900	2	–	4	4	9	19	12.7
900–1100	–	4	3	2	6	15	10.0
1100–1300	1	4	2	1	1	9	6.0
1300–1500	–	3	1	–	–	4	2.7
1500–1700	–	2	–	–	–	2	1.3
1700–1900	–	2	–	–	1	3	2.0
1900–2100	–	1	–	–	–	1	0.6
Total	**30**	**30**	**30**	**30**	**30**	**150**	**100**

Not only the monthly income, but also the data regarding the amount spent on foods was collected. About three fourths of the beneficiaries spent Rs. 300-900/-

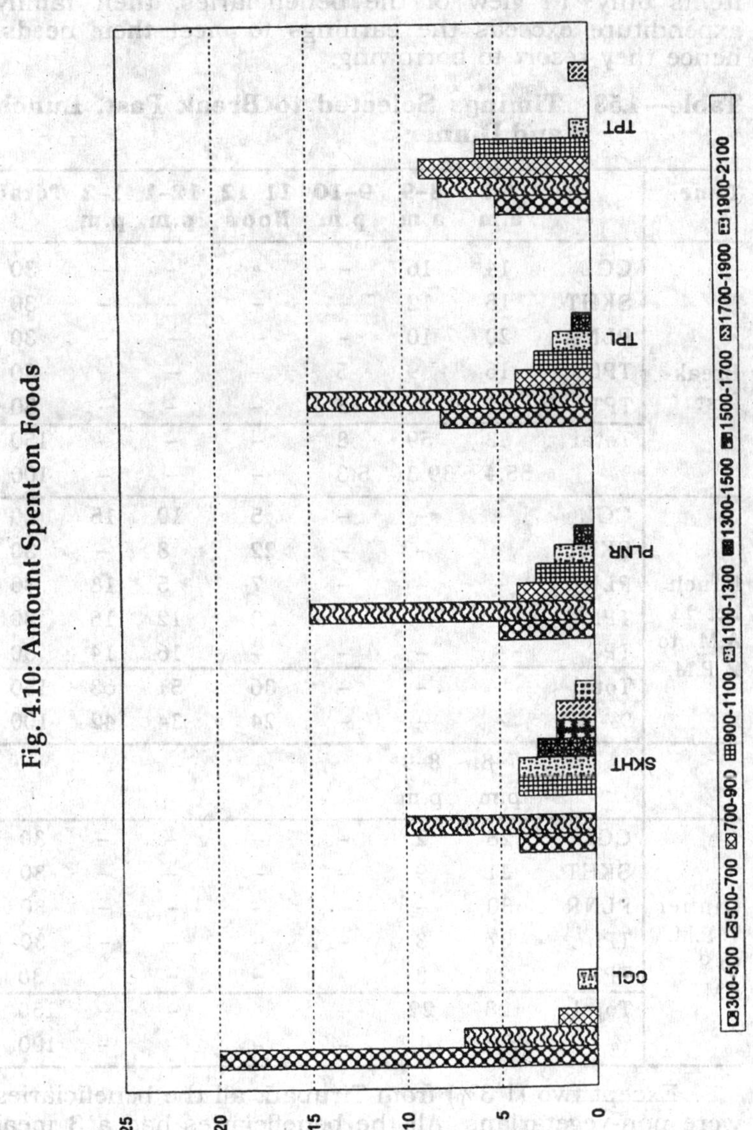

Fig. 4.10: Amount Spent on Foods

per month on food items. According to data, almost all the beneficiaries were spending their income on food items only. In view of the beneficiaries, their family expenditure exceeds the earnings to meet their needs, hence they resort to borrowing.

Table—4.53 Timings Selected to Break Fast, Lunch and Dinner

Time		7–8 a.m	8–9 a.m	9–10 p.m	11–12 Noon	12–1 p.m	1–2 p.m	Total
Break-fast	CGL	14	16	–	–	–	–	30
	SKHT	18	12	–	–	–	–	30
	PLNR	20	10	–	–	–	–	30
	TPL	16	9	5	–	–	–	30
	TPT	15	12	3	–	–	–	30
	Total	83	59	8	–	–	–	150
	%	55.4	39.3	5.3	–	–	–	100
Lunch bet 11 A.M. to 2 P.M.	CGL	–	–	–	5	10	15	30
	SKHT	–	–	–	22	8	–	30
	PLNR	–	–	–	7	5	18	30
	TPL	–	–	–	2	12	16	30
	TPT	–	–	–	–	16	14	30
	Total	–	–	–	36	51	63	150
	%	–	–	–	24	34	42	100
		7–8 p.m	8–9 p.m					
Dinner 7 P.M. to 9 PM	CGL	28	2	–	–	–	–	30
	SKHT	21	9	–	–	–	–	30
	PLNR	30	–	–	–	–	–	30
	TPL	27	3	–	–	–	–	30
	TPT	22	8	–	–	–	–	30
	Total	128	22	–	–	–	–	150
	%	85.3	14.7	–	–	–	–	100

Except two (1.3%) from Tirupati, all the beneficiaries were non-vegetarians. All the beneficiaries had a 3 meal pattern daily. Table 4.53 contains the information related to time of their meal, according to the data, half of them preferred to have their break-fast between 7.8 A.M. It shows after these hours they were busy with domestic or scheduled work. It was also observed that more than half of the beneficiaries had early lunch and dinner (i.e., 11-1 pm. and 7-8 pm.)

Table—4.54 Food Items Taken by the Respondents Daily

Food Items		Snacks (Idly, Dosa etc.)	Rice	Ragiballs	Total
Break-fast	CGL	14	16	–	30
	SKHT	7	23	–	30
	PLNR	10	20	–	30
	TPL	14	16	–	30
	TPT	16	14	–	30
	Total	61	89	–	150
	%	40.7	59.3	–	100
Lunch bet 11 A.M to 2 PM	CGL	–	24	6	30
	SKHT	–	23	7	30
	PLNR	–	30	–	30
	TPL	–	30	–	30
	TPT	–	30	–	30
	Total	–	137	13	150
	%	–	91.3	8.7	100
Dinner 7 P.M to 9 P.M	CGL	–	30	–	30
	SKHT	–	30	–	30
	PLNR	–	30	–	30
	TPL	–	30	–	30
	TPT	–	30	–	30
	Total	–	150		150
	%	–	100	–	100

Information was also collected regarding the type of food consumed by the beneficiaries, around. 60% were consuming cooked rice soaked over night in water, and the remaining took idly, dosa etc as their breakfast, and as rice being the staple food all the beneficiaries were taking rice as their lunch and dinner except 8.7 per cent of them who were take Ragi balls as their lunch due to their poverty in Chinnogottigallu and Srikalahasti.

Food habits in terms of their nutritional value, variety and quantity of intake play an important role in determining the health status, which in turn are determined by the cultural and ecological conditions. Difference in food habits, consumption level and nutritional quality are also based on their socio-economic status.

From the Table 4.55 it can be seen that 100 per cent of the beneficiaries were taking cereals and oil in their regular diet. Frequent consumption of pulses was also observed among the beneficiaries. Regarding the consumption of beverages, fruits etc, most of the respondents were observed to be consuming them weekly, monthly and occasionally, it could be due to the lack of purchasing capacity.

Table—4.55 Type and Frequency of Food Consumption

Frequency of food consumption		Cereals	Pulses	Vege-tables	Greens	Fruits	Milk &M Product	Beve-rages	Oils	Sugar & Jag-gery
Daily	CGL	30	15	30	23	8	22	15	30	16
	SKHT	30	14	14	5	6	12	9	30	9
	PLNR	30	12	30	26	1	7	4	30	9
	TPL	30	10	25	25	1	23	3	30	7
	TPT	30	10	22	9	6	25	18	30	18
	Total	150	61	121	88	22	89	49	150	59
	%	100	40.7	80.7	58.7	14.7	59.3	32.7	100	39.4
W_1	CGL	–	12	–	7	19	8	5	–	5
	SKHT	–	9	–	16	9	3	–	–	4
	PLNR	–	11	–	4	5	6	1	–	3
	TPL	–	15	–	4	25	6	4	–	2
	TPT	–	13	–	14	17	4	–	–	6
	Total	–	60	–	45	75	27	10	–	20
	%	–	40	–	30	50	18	6.6	–	13.3

(Contd...)

W_2	CGL	–	3	–	–	–	–	–	–	–
	SKHT	–	4	6	7	1	4	–	–	–
	PLNR	–	6	–	1	2	2	–	–	–
	TPL	–	5	–	–	–	–	–	–	2
	TPT	–	4	5	5	4	–	–	–	2
	Total	–	22	11	13	7	6	–	–	4
	%	–	14.7	7.3	8.7	4.7	4	–	–	2.7
W_3	CGL	–	–	–	–	–	–	–	–	–
	SKHT	–	3	10	2	–	–	–	–	–
	PLNR	–	1	–	–	–	–	–	–	–
	TPL	–	–	5	–	–	–	–	–	–
	TPT	–	3	3	2	–	–	–	–	–
	Total	–	7	18	4	1	–	–	–	–
	%	–	4.6	12	2.6	0.6	–	–	–	–
M_1	CGL	–	–	–	–	3	–	9	–	2
	SKHT	–	–	–	–	8	4	–	–	10
	PLNR	–	–	–	–	14	15	15	–	14
	TPL	–	–	–	–	2	1	1	–	11
	TPT	–	–	–	–	3	1	2	–	4
	Total	–	–	–	–	30	21	27	–	41
	%	–	–	–	–	20	14	18	–	27.3
Occa-sional	CGL	–	–	–	–	–	–	1	–	7
	SKHT	–	–	–	–	6	7	21	–	7
	PLNR	–	–	–	–	7	–	10	–	4
	TPL	–	–	–	–	2	–	22		8
	TPT	–	–	–	–	–	–	10	–	–
	Total	–	–	–	–	15	7	64	–	26
	%	–	–	–	–	10	4.7	42.7	–	17.3

W_1 = Weekly once, W_2 = Weekly twice, W_3 = Weekly thrice, M_1 = monthly once

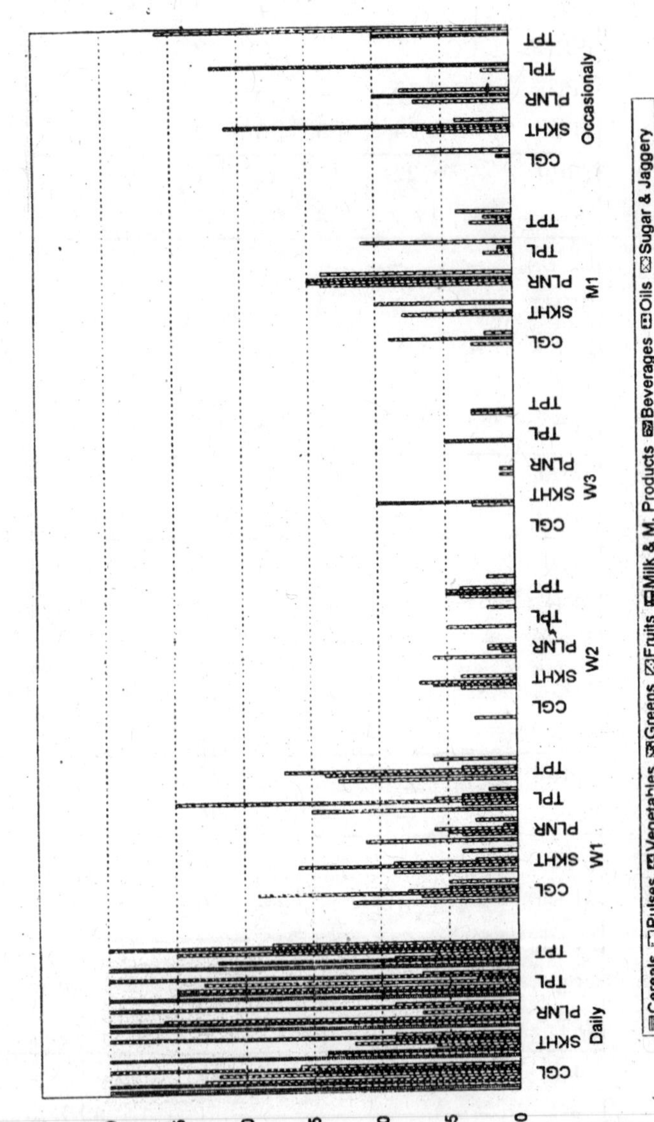

Fig. 4.11: Type and Frequency of Food Consumption

Table--4.56 Additional Foods Taken During Pregnancy

Foods	CGL	SKHT	PLNR	TPL	TPT	Total	%
Meat	10	–	4	11	1	26	17.3
Egg	14	–	5	12	7	38	25.3
Fish	–	1	–	3	1	5	3.3
Milk	6	10	8	3	4	31	20.7
Butter milk	–	–	2	–	–	2	1.3
Sweets	–	–	3	–	2	5	3.3
Greens	3	2	3	8	5	21	14.0
Dhal	1	–	3	–	–	4	2.7
Vegetables	1	–	–	4	–	5	3.3
Fruits	18	11	11	14	13	67	44.7
Nothing	7	13	11	4	10	45	30.0

During pregnancy, there should be an increase in their food-intake with required calories. Proteins, Minerals and Vitamins in an acceptable form, at a price the family can manage should form part of the meal. The foetus is small until the second half of pregnancy, and then the woman need extra food. But in study 30% of the beneficiaries were not adding any other food to their normal dies, due to their low economic status, the remaining were taking additional foods, such as fruits, egg, milk, meat etc., Knowledge, attitude and practices in relation to nutrition of pregnants was collected and presented in Table 4.57. Although most of the pregnants were aware of the need for supplements during pregnancy, they avoided certain foods due to ignorance. Almost one third of the beneficiaries avoided papaya black fruits, guava, egg, mango, etc. Avoidance of these foods is essentially a cultural practice and hence consumption of them is considered a taboo.

Fig. 4.12: Additional Foods Taken During Pregnancy

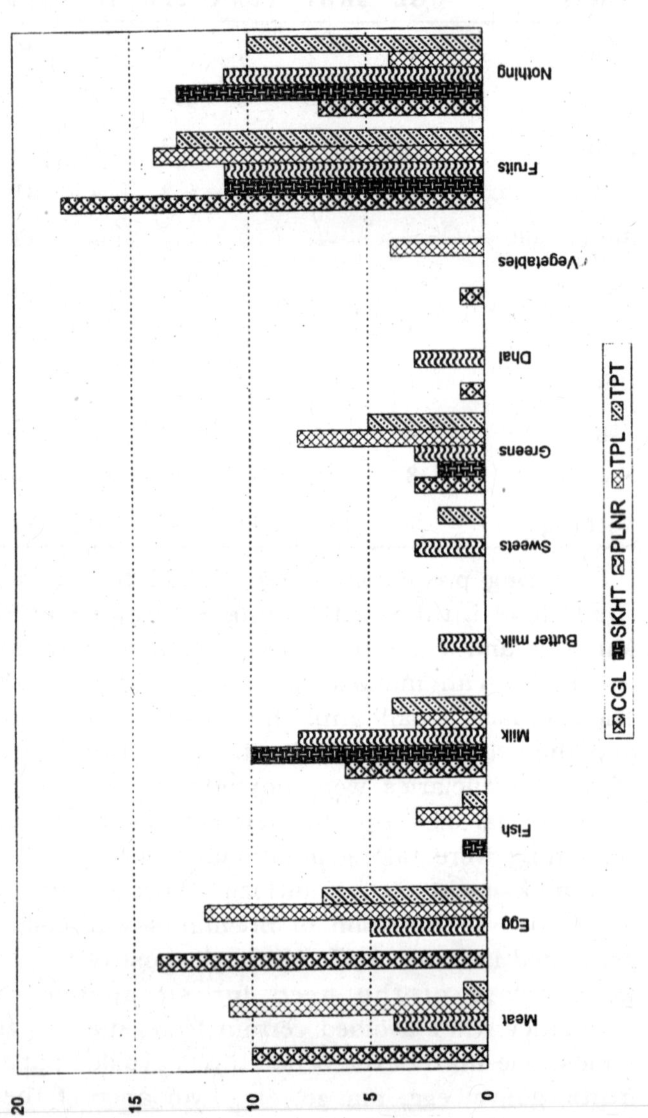

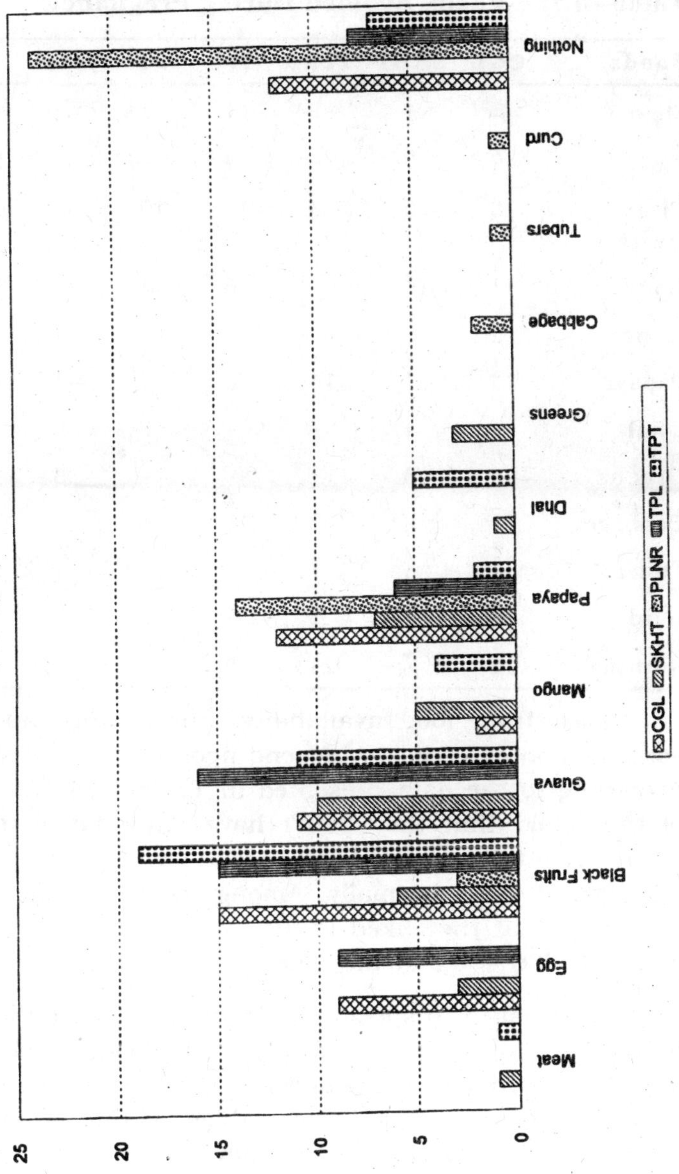

Fig. 4.13: Foods Avoided During Pregnancy

Table—4.57 Foods Avoided During Pregnancy

Foods	CGL	SKHT	PLNR	TPL	TPT	Total	%
Meat	–	1	–	–	1	2	1.3
Egg	9	3	–	9	–	21	14.0
Black fruits	15	6	3	15	19	58	38.7
Gauva	11	10	–	16	11	48	32.0
Mango	2	5	–	–	4	11	7.3
Papaya	12	7	14	6	2	41	27.3
Dhal	–	1	–	–	5	6	4.0
Greens	–	3	–	–	–	3	2.0
Cabbage	–	–	2	–	–	2	1.3
Tubers	–	–	1	–	–	1	0.7
Curd	–	–	1	–	–	1	0.7
Nothing	12	–	24	8	7	51	34.0

Apart from food availability, purchasing capacity, consumption of foods also depend upon likes and dislikes. According to the data presented in Table 4.58 one third of them told that they didn't have any change in the nature of intake during their pregnancy, they consumed all types of foods normally. Among the rest, majority of them told that they liked Fruits (36.7%), Sweets (25.3%) and Meat (26%) etc at the time of pregnancy.

When asked to specify the foods which they disliked at the time of pregnancy around 60% had no change, they consumed everything normally. The remaining didn't like the foods like Dhal, Vegetables, Potato, Cabbage, Sweets etc., during their pregnancy.

As ours is a traditional society, women are expected to take food after all the family members have finished taking their food. But in the study, (Table 4.59) it is noted that nearly 60% of the beneficiaries were taking food along with other family members and even 28.7% of them were taking whenever they felt hungry or when they finished their work. Still it was observed that 13.3% of them were taking food after all the family members, even though they were pregnants.

Table—4.58 Food Liked/Disliked During Pregnancy

Food Item	Liked						
	CGL	SKHT	PLNR	TPL	TPT	Total	%
Meat	12	4	8	12	2	38	26.0
Fish	–	–	–	3	–	3	2.0
Sweets	3	–	16	11	8	38	25.3
Fruits	14	4	15	11	11	55	36.7
Milk & Milk products	–	1	3	–	–	4	2.7
Dhal	–	–	1	–	1	2	1.3
Greens	2	2	–	–	2	6	4.0
Vegetables	2	–	2	–	–	4	2.7
Drumstics	–	2	–	–	–	2	1.3
Mango	–	1	–	–	–	1	0.7
Brinjal	–	–	–	–	–	–	–
Potato	–	1	–	–	–	1	0.7
Green plantain	–	2	–	–	–	2	1.3
Cabbage	–	–	–	–	–	–	–
Rice	–	–	–	–	–	–	–
Nothing	10	16	4	7	14	51	34.0

(Contd...)

Food Item	Disliked						
	CGL	SKHT	PLNR	TPL	TPT	Total	%
Meat	–	–	–	–	3	3	2.0
Fish	–	–	–	–	–	–	–
Sweets	3	–	–	–	2	5	3.3
Fruits	–	2	–	–	–	1	0.7
Milk & Milk products	–	2	1	–	2	5	3.3
Dhal	10	1	3	7	2	23	15.3
Greens	–	–	2	–	–	2	1.3
Vegetables	2	–	3	–	1	6	4.0
Drumstics	–	1	–	–	–	1	0.7
Mango	–	–	–	–	–	–	–
Brinjal	–	1	–	–	–	1	0.7
Potato	–	–	3	4	–	7	4.7
Green plantain	–	–	–	–	–	–	–
Cabbage	–	–	–	7	–	7	4.7
Rice	–	–	–	–	1	1	0.7
Nothing	20	21	16	15	20	92	61.3

Relatively higher percent (24.7%) of pregnant women had the habit of chewing betelnut leaves. About half of the Thamballapalle beneficiaries had even habit of eating mud or chalk 27.3% of the beneficiaries did not have any such habits (Table 4.60).

Majority of the beneficiaries finished their break-fast and dinner before 8° clock, and lunch in between 1-2 P.M. (Table 4.61). Rice, sambar, vegetable preparation, rasam and butter milk were the usual items consumed

Fig. 4.14: Mode of Eating

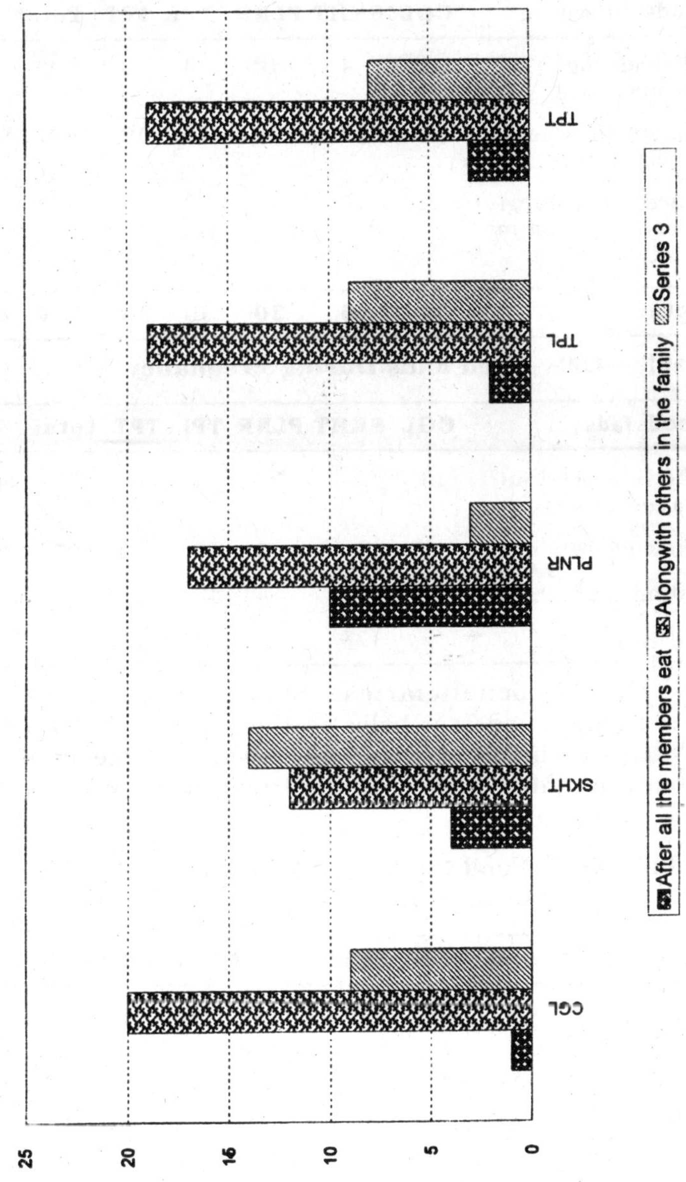

Table—4.59 Mode of Eating

Mode of eating	CGL	SKHT	PLNR	TPL	TPT	Total	%
After all the members eat	1	4	10	2	3	20	13.3
Alongwith others in the family	20	12	17	19	19	87	58.0
When I feel hungry/ after I finish all my work	9	14	3	9	8	43	28.7
Total	**30**	**30**	**30**	**30**	**30**	**150**	**100**

Table—4.60 Food Fads During Pregnancy

Food fads	CGL	SKHT	PLNR	TPL	TPT	Total	%
Chewing betalnut leaves	13	–	20	1	3	37	24.7
Chewing betelnut	1	–	5	19	2	27	18.0
Eating mud/chalk	1	–	–	17	2	20	13.3
Nothing	3	27	2	1	8	41	27.3

by all the beneficiaries. Seven per cent of the beneficiaries had ragi balls as their lunch. The number of items included in the meal depend on the time and money available. Almost all the beneficiaries were regular rice eaters.

Table—4.61 Food Consumed Previous day of the Data Collection

	Food Item	CGL	SKHT	PLNR	TPL	TPT	Total	%
Break-fast	Rice with water	19	19	17	16	14	85	56.7
	Tiffen (Idly, Dosa)	11	11	13	14	16	65	43.3
	Total	**30**	**30**	**30**	**30**	**30**	**150**	**100**

(Contd...)

	Rice	30	20	30	30	29	139	92.6
	Vegetables	30	19	30	29	30	138	92.0
	Rasam	15	9	8	19	17	68	45.3
	Buttermilk	3	–	5	9	12	19	12.7
	Saambar	–	9	–	7	6	22	14.7
	Ragiballs	–	10	–	–	1	11	7.3
Lunch	GLV	–	4	–	–	4	8	5.3
	Egg	–	2	–	–	–	2	1.3
	Fish	–	1	–	–	–	1	0.7
	Meat	–	1	–	–	1	2	1.3
	Chutney	–	1	–	1	–	2	1.3
	Rice	30	30	30	30	30	150	100.0
	Vegetables	30	25	30	29	30	144	96.0
	Rasam	17	10	15	–	22	64	42.7
	Buttermilk	2	3	5	10	8	28	18.7
	Saambar	–	9	3	–	5	17	11.3
Dinner	GLV	–	5	–	3	4	12	8.0
	Egg	–	5	–	–	–	5	3.3
	Fish	–	1	–	–	–	1	0.7
	Meat	–	1	–	–	3	4	2.7
	Chutney	–	1	–	22	–	23	15.3

The information collected regarding post-reproductive performance (Table 4.62) indicates that there was only one premature birth, 2% of still births and 4.6% of miscarriages out of 150 respondents. The information related to number of children, 71.4% of them had one or two children 12.6% were having 3-6 children and there were no children yet for the rest of the beneficiaries. Of the total pregnants nearly half of them were in their 2nd pregnancy and it was even the 5th and 6th pregnancy for two beneficiaries.

Table—4.62 Post Re-productive Performance

Post reproductive performance	CGL	SKHT	PLNR	TPL	TPT	Total	%
Miscarriage	–	1	–	4	2	7	4.6
Premature births	–	–	–	–	1	1	0.7
Still births (at 8th month)	1	–	–	1	1	3	2.0
Living Children							
1–2	23	19	19	23	23	107	71.7
3–4	2	5	6	2	2	17	11.3
5–6	–	–	1	1	–	2	1.3
No Children yet	5	6	4	4	5	24	16.0
Total	**30**	**30**	**30**	**30**	**30**	**150**	**100**
Total no. of pregnancies							
One	5	6	4	4	5	24	16.0
Two	13	16	11	14	13	67	44.6
Three	10	6	8	11	7	42	28.0
Four	2	2	6	1	4	15	10.0
Five	–	–	–	–	1	1	0.7
Six	–	–	1	–	–	1	0.7
Total	**30**	**30**	**30**	**30**	**30**	**150**	**100**

Participation in the Feeding Programme

All the beneficiaries were participating in feeding programme conducted by ICDS except 2 members from Tirupati and one from Kalahasthi Project, as there was no one to get SNF daily. Except 4% of the beneficiaries, rest of them collected the SNF daily. The amount of SNF they get 135 grms of Normal food or weaning food daily. The amount of SNF they consumed is presented in Table 4.63.

Table—4.63 Quantity of SNF Consumption During Pregnancy

Quantity (in grms)	CGL	SKHT	PLNR	TPL	TPT	Total	%
Nil	-	3	5	-	11	19	12.9
10–50	-	6	-	-	3	9	6.1
50–90	-	12	25	-	14	51	34.7
90–135	30	8	-	30	-	68	46.3
Total	**30**	**29**	**30**	**30**	**28**	**147**	**100**

Although the quality of food was good, but acceptability of such food was rather poor, because of monotonous taste, same preparation every day, fear of stomach pain, indigestion etc were the main complaints especially by the beneficiaries of Sri Kalahasthi Project and Tirupati. 46.3 per cent of the beneficiaries were consuming the whole amount of SNF given to them.

Consumption of Folic Acid Tablets

Investigation revealed that a great number of pregnant women were covered under antenatal care. Almost all the beneficiaries were consuming Iron and Folic acid tablets given at 7 month (30 tablets), 8th month (30 and 9th month (40 tablets) by AWW, except 5 beneficiaries from Kalahasthi, who told that they were not taking these tablets because AW personnel have not distributed them properly.

Details Pertaining to Lactating Mothers

The other principal beneficiaries of the ICDS scheme are lactating mothers. Nursing mothers during the period when child is 0-6 months old, also come under the purview of the scheme. The type of services provided to lactating mothers are supplementary nutrition consisting of about 500 calories and 25 grams of protein, Health check-up, Referral services and Health and nutrition education etc.

A very high rate of infant mortality in India is further characterised by the fact that maximum infant deaths take place in the first week of life. It is, therefore, obvious that post-natal care is also an important aspect of health care system particularly in rural and tribal areas.

Table—4.64 Knowledge about Services of AWC

Services	CGL	SKHT	PLNR	TPL	TPT	Total	%
Health check-up	18	9	14	15	15	71	71
Immunization	20	20	20	20	20	100	100
Supplementary food	20	20	20	20	20	100	100
Non formal pre-school education	20	20	20	20	20	100	100
Nutrition & Health education	15	10	10	11	10	56	56
Referral services	11	9	12	10	10	52	52

The study revealed that all the beneficiaries were aware of the various services rendered by AWC, when asked to specify the services all of them were aware of Immunization, supplementary food and pre-school education. Half of the beneficiaries were aware of Nutrition and Health education and Referral services. Thus it indicates that, the AWC was mostly known as nutritious noon meal centre for pre-school children.

The Immunization service is appreciated by all the beneficiaries and was utilized for their families, followed by supplementary nutrition. (Table 4.65) For a Lactating mother, from delivery upto six months, she gets 135 gms of SNF, either normal or weaning food regularly. Usually if she is anaemic she should get folic acid tablets for the above period along with SNF: (prescribed in the ICDS

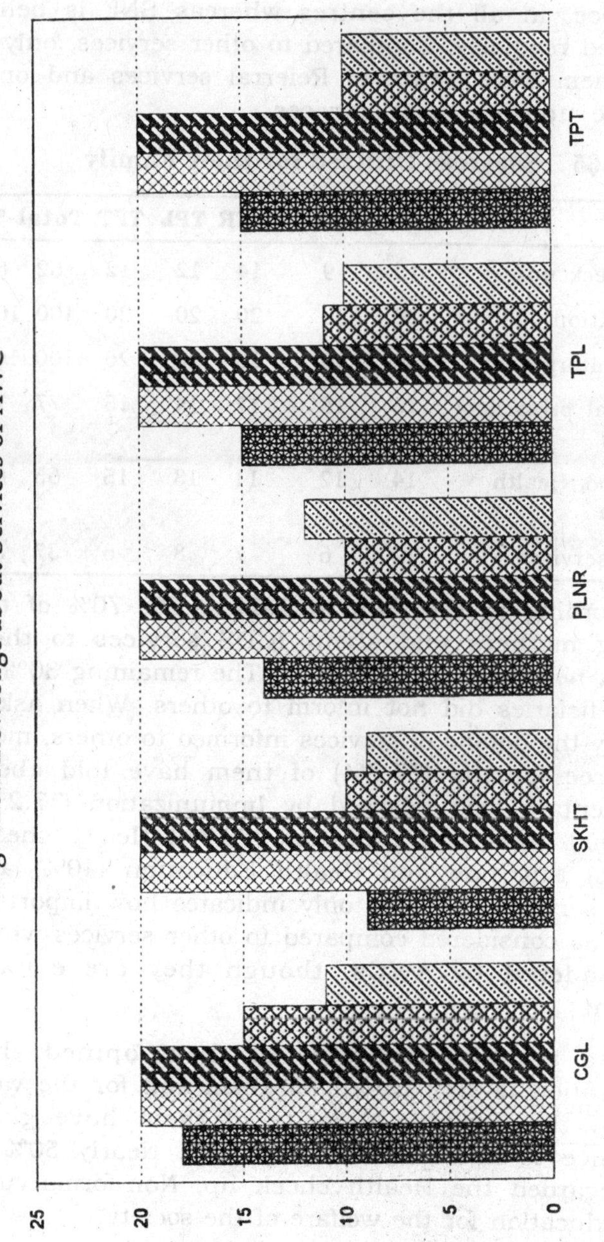

Fig. 4.15: Knowledge about Services of AWC

manual). But the distribution of folic acid tablets is not in practice, in all the centres whereas SNF is being distributed regularly. Compared to other services, only a few of them were aware of Referral services and only they were utilizing these services.

Table—4.65 Services Utilized for their Family

Services	CGL	SKHT	PLNR	TPL	TPT	Total	%
Health check up	15	9	14	12	12	62	62
Immunization	20	20	20	20	20	100	100
Supplementary food	20	20	20	20	20	100	100
Non formal pre-school education	16	15	17	14	15	77	77
Nutrition & Health education	14	12	11	13	15	65	65
Referral services	10	6	7	8	6	37	37

According to the data in Table 4.66, 70% of the lactating mothers told about ICDS services to their relatives, neighbours and friends. The remaining 30% of the beneficiaries did not inform to others. When asked to specify the details of services informed to others, more than three fourths (77.8%) of them have told about supplementary food followed by Immunization (77.2%), Non-formal pre-school education (73.7%) Health check-up (50%) Nutrition and Health Education (40%) and Referral services (20%). It only indicates how important the food is considered compared to other services which were rendered by AWCs, though they are equally important.

Data reveals that 70% of them opined that Immunization is very useful for them and for the well-being of the society. Majority of them have given importance to Immunization and SNF. Nearly 50% of them regarded the Health check up, Non-formal pre-school education for the welfare of the society.

Table—4.66 Information Given to Others About Services

Information about services	CGL	SKHT	PLNR	TPL	TPT	Total	%
Yes	14	12	15	15	14	70	70
No	6	8	5	5	6	30	30
Total	20	20	20	20	20	100	100
If Yes, to							
Neighbours	5	4	9	6	6	30	42.8
Relatives	8	5	5	7	6	31	44.3
Friends	1	3	1	2	2	9	12.9

According to findings presented in Table 4.67, 63% of the beneficiaries extended their help to AWW in taking the children to AWC, at the time of vaccination, in conducting meetings and also in sending the children daily for pre-school. The remaining have not helped the AWW in any way. The reasons expressed, nearly 60% of them were busy with domestic work, followed by 29.7%% who had no interest to involve in AWC activities, and the remaining (13.5%) told that they didn't extend their help to AWW because she didn't ask for help.

Table—4.67 Help Given by Beneficiaries to AWW

Help given by beneficiaries to AWW	CGL	SKHT	PLNR	TPL	TPT	Total	%
Yes	12	9	14	13	15	63	63
No	8	11	6	7	5	37	37
Total	**20**	**20**	**20**	**20**	**20**	**100**	**100**
If Yes, Type of help							
In taking children to AWC for vaccination	7	5	10	7	10	39	61.9
In conducting meetings	5	4	4	6	5	24	38.1
Total	**12**	**9**	**14**	**13**	**15**	**63**	**100**

(Contd...)

Help given by beneficiaries to AWW	CGL	SKHT	PLNR	TPL	TPT	Total	%
Reasons for not extended							
Busy with domestic work	5	5	4	5	2	21	56.8
Lack of interest	3	4	1	1	2	11	29.7
AWW didn't ask	–	2	1	1	1	5	13.5
Total	**8**	**11**	**6**	**7**	**5**	**37**	**100**

Further investigation reveals that all the beneficiaries in Chinnagottigalu, palamaneru, Tamballapalle and only 38.7% (12) beneficiaries of Tirupati project have taken lead to help the AWW in conducting meetings, organizing Mahila Mandals, SNF distribution etc. None of the beneficiaries from Kalahasthi project have taken lead to conduct AWC activities, again lack of time, interest, ignorance etc were the reasons expressed by them.

HEALTH SERVICES

The ICDS programme represents a major effort on health check-up immunization and referral services to improve the health and nutritional status of 0-6 years old children, pregnant and nursing mothers. To know their knowledge about different health services rendered through AWC, data was collected and presented in Table 4.68-4.71.

Table—4.68 Mothers Awareness About Different Health Services

Services	CGL	SKHT	PLNR	TPL	TPT	Total	%
Health check-up							
Pregnant	35	25	40	43	22	165	66.0
Lactating mother	35	25	40	43	26	169	67.6
Children	35	25	40	43	28	171	68.4
Immunization							
Pregnant	50	50	50	50	50	250	100
Children	50	50	50	50	50	250	100

(Contd...)

Referral services							
Pregnant	12	10	40	40	17	119	47.6
Lactating mother	–	–	–	–	–	–	–
Children	–	–	–	–	–	–	–

Around 70% of the respondents were aware of Health check-up. Referral services that is extended to pregnant women, only 47.6% knew about it, where as for lactating mothers and children, none of them have any idea abou referral services. On the whole immunization is the only service which was known to 100 per cent of the members of respondents.

Table—4.69 Awareness of Pregnant Women About Different Health Services

Services	CGL	SKHT	PLNR	TPL	TPT	Total	%
Health check-up							
Pregnant	25	15	20	19	20	99	66.0
Lactating mother	20	14	20	19	20	93	62.0
Children	20	18	20	19	21	98	65.3
Immunization							
Pregnant	30	30	30	30	30	150	100
Children	30	30	30	30	30	150	100
Referral services							
Pregnant	10	8	12	14	13	57	38
Lactating mother	10	8	12	14	13	57	38
Children	10	8	12	14	13	57	38

With regard to the pregnant women around 65% of them told that they knew about the health check-up for children, pregnant and lactating women. All of them were aware of the immunization which is given to pregnant women and children. Regarding referral services only 38%, were aware of it which is given to pregnant women, lactating mothers and children.

Table—4.70 Awareness of Lactating Mothers About Different Health Services

Services	CGL	SKHT	PLNR	TPL	TPT	Total	%
Health check-up							
Pregnant	18	13	18	14	15	78	78
Lactating mother	10	13	9	8	7	47	47
Immunization							
Pregnant	20	20	20	20	20	100	100
Children	20	20	20	20	20	100	100
Referral services							
Pregnant	9	6	8	10	11	44	44
Lactating mother	9	6	5	8	7	40	40
Children	9	6	8	6	10	39	39

Almost 65% of the lactating mothers were aware of different health services, rendered through AWC. All of them were aware of the immunization which was given to pregnant women and children. With regard to the referral services, all the three categories of beneficiaries such as mothers, pregnant women and lactating mothers have more or less same awareness.

The level of awareness about general health check up has been observed among the beneficiaries as satisfactory (Table 4.71). On the whole about three-fourths (71.6%) of them were aware about general health check-up. When asked them to specify the nature of health check-up done by ANM, more than 50% of them told, that the ANM checks eyes, nails, tongue, weight and B.P. 100% of them told, she checks B.P and she also tests the urine and blood for some infections.

Mothers at risk were women who have had abortions, didn't gain weight during pregnancy, have had

Table—4.71 Awareness About General Health Check-up for Pregnant Women

Awareness	CGL	SKHT	PLNR	TPL	TPT	Total	%
Yes	80	54	78	80	66	358	71.6
No	20	46	22	20	34	142	28.4
Total	**100**	**100**	**100**	**100**	**100**	**500**	**100**
If yes, nature of check-up							
Checking							
Eyes	80	34	48	25	66	253	70.67
Nails	60	20	20	25	66	191	53.4
Tongue	50	20	20	25	66	181	50.1
Weight	80	54	78	80	66	358	100.0
BP	80	54	78	80	66	358	100.0
Urine	80	54	78	80	66	358	100.0
Blood	80	54	78	80	66	358	100.0

frequent deliveries, were suffering with chronic diseases, were anaemic, were handicapped, and had early and late pregnancies etc (Table 4.72). According to data, nearly 15 mothers, 10 pregnant and 10 lactating mothers were not aware of anything about mothers at risk.

Among the mothers of pre-school children, majority of them referred that anaemia and women and women who have had abortions and frequent deliveries was a risky condition. Similar pattern was observed even among the pregnant women. But majority of the lactating mothers opined that the women who have had abortions were in a risky condition and those who will have first delivery were also categorised as mothers at risk. One respondent from Tirupati expressed that of the pregnant women who is short in height is also catergorised as mother at risk.

Table—4.72 Awareness About Mothers who are at Risk

Mothers who are at risk	Mothers (n = 250)						
	CGL	SKHT	PLNR	TPL	TPT	Total	%
Those who had abortions	40	21	40	43	26	170	68.0
Those with no weight gain during pregnancy	35	10	20	23	12	100	40.0
Those who have frequent deliveries	30	15	39	40	13	137	54.8
Those suffering with chronic disease	25	8	38	13	12	96	38.4
Those who are anaemic	29	31	32	40	28	160	64.0
Those who are handicapped	30	12	6	21	7	76	30.4
Early and late pregnancies	8	4	3	6	12	33	13.2
Those who didn't have TT	4	4	3	5	6	22	8.8
Those who are not having exercise (work)	20	18	19	21	20	98	39.2
First delivery	10	12	14	18	17	71	28.4
Those who are short in height	–	–	–	–	–	–	–

(Contd...)

Mothers who are at risk	Pregnant Women (n=150)						
	CGL	SKHT	PLNR	TPL	TPT	Total	%
Those who had abortions	25	15	30	29	12	111	74.0
Those with no weight gain during pregnancy	15	3	–	8	9	35	23.3
Those who have frequent deliveries	25	8	22	29	10	94	62.7
Those suffering with chronic disease	15	2	–	8	9	34	22.7
Those who are anaemic	24	9	25	28	15	101	67.3
Those who are handicapped	10	–	10	12	–	32	21.3
Early and late pregnancies	19	12	14	14	12	71	47.3
Those who didn't have TT	6	–	–	–	2	8	5.3
Those who are not having exercise (work)	14	13	9	11	8	55	36.7
First delivery	12	10	11	10	8	51	34.0
Those who are short in height	–	–	–	–	–	–	–

(Contd...)

Mothers who are at risk	Lactating Mother (n=100)						
	CGL	SKHT	PLNR	TPL	TPT	Total	%
Those who had abortions	20	20	15	14	16	85	85
Those with no weight gain during pregnancy	10	8	9	–	8	35	35
Those who have frequent deliveries	11	10	9	8	6	44	44
Those suffering with chronic disease	6	14	8	8	7	43	43
Those who are anaemic	3	2	20	13	14	52	52
Those who are handicapped	8	9	–	–	–	17	17
Early and late pregnancies	9	8	8	12	12	49	49
Those who didn't have TT	3	2	–	–	–	5	5
Those who are not having exercise (work)	10	9	7	9	8	43	43
First delivery	14	10	8	8	7	47	47
Those who are short in height	–	–	–	–	1	1	1

Table 4.73 reveals the utilization of health services during their pregnancy. Around 65 per cent of mothers of pre-school children consulted the doctor either at private or Government Hospital. Among these 51.8% went to hospital once in every month 21% of them consulted the doctor once in a week.

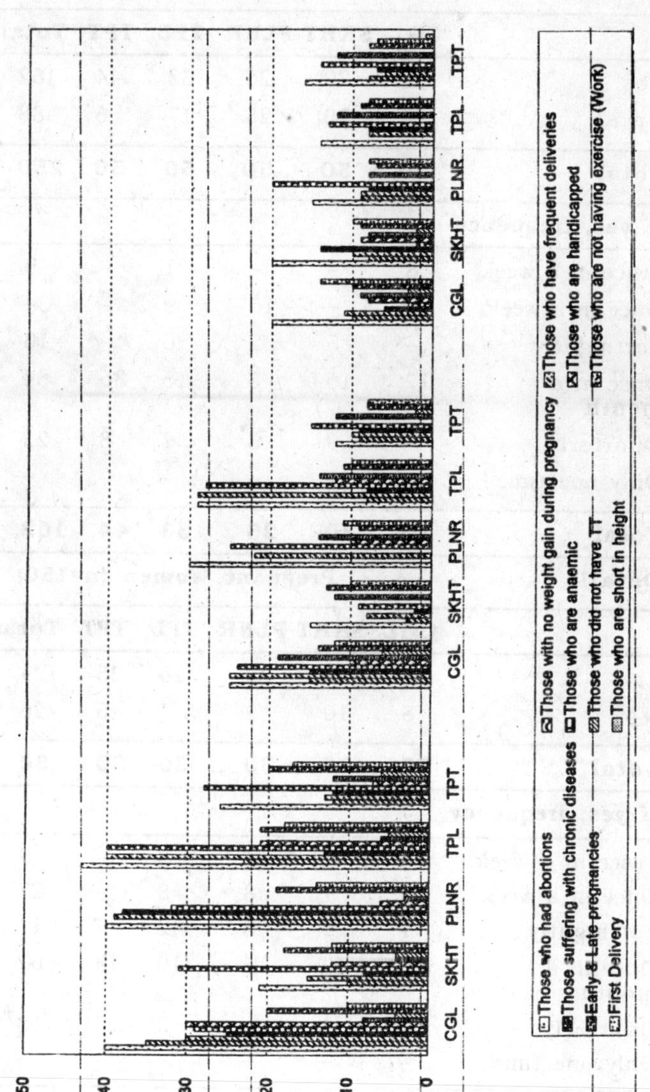

Fig. 4.16: Awareness About Mothers Who are at Risk

Table—4.73 Those Who Used Health Services During Pregnancy

Details	Mothers (n = 250)						
	CGL	**SKHT**	**PLNR**	**TPL**	**TPT**	**Total**	**%**
Yes	30	30	25	33	44	162	64.8
No	20	20	25	17	6	88	35.2
Total	**50**	**50**	**50**	**50**	**50**	**250**	**100**
If yes, frequency							
Twice in a week	8	–	–	1	–	9	5.6
Once in a week	10	–	15	9	–	34	21.0
Fortnightly	–	5	2	6	–	13	8.0
Once in a month	12	16	5	15	36	84	51.8
Quarterly	–	9	3	2	8	22	13.6
Only one time	–	–	–	–	–	–	–
Total	**30**	**30**	**25**	**33**	**44**	**162**	**100**
Details	**Pregnant Women (n=150)**						
	CGL	**SKHT**	**PLNR**	**TPL**	**TPT**	**Total**	**%**
Yes	25	20	28	26	25	124	82.7
No	5	10	2	4	5	26	17.3
Total	**30**	**30**	**30**	**30**	**30**	**150**	**100**
If yes, frequency							
Twice in a week	4	1	–	3	–	8	6.4
Once in a week	10	1	8	8	–	27	21.8
Fortnightly	1	2	5	2	4	14	11.6
Once in a month	10	13	15	10	14	62	50.0
Quarterly	–	3	–	3	7	13	10.5
Only one time	–	–	–	–	–	–	–
Total	**25**	**20**	**28**	**26**	**25**	**124**	**100**

(Contd...)

Details	Mothers (n = 250)						
	CGL	SKHT	PLNR	TPL	TPT	Total	%
Yes	18	17	15	14	17	81	81
No	2	3	5	6	3	19	19
Total	**20**	**20**	**20**	**20**	**20**	**100**	**100**
If yes, frequency							
Twice in a week	3	1	2	2	–	8	9.9
Once in a week	4	3	3	6	1	17	21.0
Fortnightly	–	2	4	–	–	6	7.4
Once in a month	8	7	6	5	13	39	48.1
Quarterly	2	3	–	–	3	8	9.9
Only one time	1	1	–	1	–	3	3.7
Total	**18**	**17**	**15**	**14**	**17**	**81**	**100**

83% per cent of pregnant women consulted doctor for various reasons. Half of them consulted once in a month, followed by 21.8%, who went to hospital once in a week.

Among the lactating mothers also, majority of them have utilized the health services monthly once. Twenty one per cent have consulted the doctor once in a week. On the whole the utilization of health services during their pregnancy was considerably good.

According to Table 4.74 out of the total beneficiaries, who used the health services, nearly half of them (47%) have consulted the doctor about their weakness during pregnancy. Relatively a higher per cent of beneficiaries (53%) told that they didn't any problem, but they consulted the doctor just to know the position of the baby in the womb. Out of 47% of them, 25.4% of the respondents were

Table—4.74 Health Problems During Pregnancy

Health problems	CGL	SKHT	PLNR	TPL	TPT	Total	%
Anaemia	32	17	16	21	41	127	25.4
Swelling legs	4	4	3	4	2	17	3.4
Fever	6	1	14	4	6	31	6.2
Cough	7	–	10	11	4	32	6.4
Stomach pain	–	5	–	–	–	5	1.0
BP	2	4	3	2	1	12	2.4
Asthma	–	2	–	2	–	4	0.8
Body pains	–	1	–	–	–	1	0.2
Pain during urination	–	1	2	2	1	6	1.2
Nothing	49	65	52	54	45	265	53.0
Total	**100**	**100**	**100**	**100**	**100**	**500**	**100**

suffering with anaemia, fever, cough, swelling of legs, stomach pain, high blood pressure, asthma, body pains, pain during urination etc, were the health problems for the remaining beneficiaries.

Table—4.75 The Place Where the Children Got Treatment

Place	CGL	SKHT	PLNR	TPL	TPT	Total	%
AWC	8	2	15	9	13	47	10.1
Private clinic	26	38	34	28	43	169	36.3
Govt. Hospital	6	13	5	3	7	34	7.3
PHC	10	3	16	26	15	70	15.0
AWC & Private clinic	7	14	8	4	6	39	8.4
AWE and Govt. Hospital	5	8	–	–	4	17	3.6
AWC & PHC	13	2	12	12	–	39	8.4
Go for mantras	3	2	2	4	3	14	3.0
No problem so far	13	8	4	9	3	37	7.9
Total	**91**	**90**	**96**	**95**	**94**	**466**	**100**

Information was also collected on the place where their children were treated when they fell ill. More than one-thirds of the beneficiaries told that their children were given treatment in private clinics, 15% of them told that they went to PHC. Still some of the beneficiaries told that they went to doctor for treatment and they also have faith on mantras, so they went for mantras when their children fell ill.

Table 4.76 shows the health problems of the children, majority of the children suffered with Fever (59.9%) followed by Cough (48.5%), Anaemia (24.5%) and Diarrhoea (35%). As children are more prone to health problems, stomach pain, cold, head ache, vomiting, scores etc were the common diseases among all the children of beneficiaries.

Table—4.76 Health Problems of Children

Problems	CGL	SKHT	PLNR	TPL	TPT	Total	%
Fever	69	88	29	41	52	279	59.9
Cough	15	71	35	60	45	226	48.5
Anaemia	22	–	17	29	46	114	24.5
Diarrhoea	12	37	44	40	30	163	35.0
Stomach pain	3	6	21	–	3	33	7.1
Cold	34	16	32	25	29	136	29.2
Headache	8	4	7	–	–	19	4.1
Constipation	4	2	–	–	–	6	1.3
Joint pains	2	1	–	–	–	3	0.6
Vomiting	17	1	15	11	–	44	9.4
Sores	11	2	–	–	2	15	3.2
Pus in the ear	2	1	3	–	–	6	1.3
Not taken food properly	–	–	2	–	1	3	0.6

Basic good health is essential for better living. So, to achieve "Health for all by 2000 AD" and to provide primary health care to all, all the health professionals, social workers, agencies and institutions should co-ordinate their activities to train personnel and educate the masses with singleness of purpose. We cannot manage our lives and our health in isolation from the rest without community action. Since the concept of preventive care of diseases is lacking in people and providers, intensive education, on salient aspects of preventive measures may be provided to one and all on a continuous basis.

PROFILE OF ANGANWADI WORKERS

Anganwadi, as a term, denotes a place for women and children from a specific category, where services related to nutrition, health, and education are provided. Anganwadi worker is the kingpin of the ICDS programme whose success rests to a large extent on her ability and capacity to perform her role and responsibilities effectively. Anganwadi worker is expected to be a local woman, is required to perform the following duties:

1. Community survey and enlisting beneficiaries;
2. Supplementary feeding of 0-6 years of children, pregnant and nursing mothers;
3. Health and nutrition education to women, children and the community, population education to women and parents and community education;
4. Non-formal pre-school education of the children between 3 and 6 years of age;
5. Primary health care and first aid to children under six years, pregnant and nursing mothers;
6. Detection of impairments among children in the early stage and help in prevention of disabilities;
7. Contacting the parents of children coming to the Anganwadi through home visits and enlisting their participation in the programme;

8. Assisting health staff in immunization and health check-up;
9. Referral services for severely under-nourished/ mal-nourished, sick and at-risk children, and cases of communicable diseases and children with impairments;
10 Maintaining records/registers of the Anganwadi centre;
11. Maintaining liaison with other institutions in the village/urban slums.

Apart from above said responsibilities, the Anganwadi worker has to perform the following additional responsibilities.

Conducting annual village level educational survey along with school teachers, taking care of DWCRA groups, where the schemes are being implemented, helping the extension staff in demonstrations on NHE and she also acts as a village rehabilitation worker by creating awareness for early detection of disability, its prevention etc.

The details pertaining to Anganwadi workers (50) of five ICDS projects have been presented in Tables 4.77 to 4.105.

Table—4.77 Age of the Respondents

Age in years	CGL	SKHT	PLNR	TPL	TPT	Total	%
20–25	5	–	4	2	–	11	22.0
25–30	3	–	3	1	–	7	14.0
30–35	1	1	3	2	3	10	20.0
35–40	1	2	–	1	3	7	14.0
40–45	–	5	–	4	4	13	26.0
45–50	–	2	–	–	–	2	4.0
Total	**10**	**10**	**10**	**10**	**10**	**50**	**100**

Age is one of the important factor as it influences the capacity to work. According to the NIPCCD'S Manual on Integrated Child Development Services., the required age limit for an Anganwadi worker (AWW) is between 25-41 years. But the enquiries revealed that of the 30% of the respondents were above 40 years of age (Table 4.77).

Table—4.78 Religion of the Respondents

Religion	CGL	SKHT	PLNR	TPL	TPT	Total	%
Hindu	8	8	9	8	8	41	82
Christian	1	2	–	2	1	6	12
Muslim	1	–	1	–	1	3	6
Total	**10**	**10**	**10**	**10**	**10**	**50**	**100**

Religion is an institution that instils a particular philosophy of life in an individual. Table 4.78 shows the distribution of the AWWs by their religion. Among the respondents, Hindus form the majority (82%) and the remaining 12% and 6% of the respondents were Christians and Muslims respectively.

Table—4.79 Caste of the Respondents

Caste	CGL	SKHT	PLNR	TPL	TPT	Total	%
Farward Caste	6	2	3	5	6	22	44
Backward Caste	4	8	7	5	2	26	52
Scheduled Caste	–	–	–	–	2	2	4
Total	**10**	**10**	**10**	**10**	**10**	**50**	**100**

Table 4.79 shows the respondents caste, according to the data, relatively higher percentage of respondents belong to backward and scheduled castes. Only 44% of them were from forward caste category. The reason could be the hesitation to take up a less remunerative employment among the forward caste category.

Table—4.80 Marital Status of the Respondents

Marital Status	CGL	SKHT	PLNR	TPL	TPT	Total	%
Unmarried	6	1	3	2	–	12	24
Married	4	7	7	8	9	35	70
Widow	–	2	–	–	1	3	6
Total	**10**	**10**	**10**	**10**	**10**	**50**	**100**

Marital status is an important factor in the context of work relationship of the AWW. Seventy six per cent of them were married (Table 4.80). However, 6% of them were widows, all the respondents irrespective of their marital status, have taken up jobs as AWWs as a source of additional income.

Table—4.81 Educational Qualifications of the Respondents

Education	CGL	SKHT	PLNR	TPL	TPT	Total	%
8th class	–	1	–	–	–	1	2
9th class	–	1	–	–	–	1	2
10th class	3	7	6	7	8	31	62
Intermediate	4	–	3	2	1	10	20
Graduation	3	1	1	1	1	7	14
Total	**10**	**10**	**10**	**10**	**10**	**50**	**100**

Educational qualifications are flexible for the appointment of AWW, since the emphasis is on local women. According to the data in Table 4.81, 62% of the respondents completed their 10th class. Four per cent of them have discontinued their education at 8th and 9th classes only. It is interesting to note that 14% of the respondents even studied up to graduation.

The study of the AWW necessitates an enquiry into their experience because it forms special significance as far as efficiency is concerned. Data in Table 4.82 reveals about the service experience of AWWs. According to the data about one-thirds of the respondents had only 3-5 years of experience, followed by 24% who have been working for 13-15 years.

Table—4.82 Total Length of Service of the Respondents

Service in Years	CGL	SKHT	PLNR	TPL	TPT	Total	%
3–5	9	–	5	3	–	17	34.0
5–7	–	–	5	–	3	8	16.0
7–9	1	–	–	1	–	2	4.0
9–11	–	–	–	2	3	5	10.0
11–13	–	2	–	1	3	6	12.0
13–15	–	8	–	3	1	12	24.0
Total	**10**	**10**	**10**	**10**	**10**	**50**	**100**

With regard to the recruitment of the anganwadi workers, all the respondents were selected through an interview.

Details About the Training Programmes Attended

The data regarding the training programmes attended by AWWs revealed that all the AWWs had undergone orientation or job course training and also the inservice training which is also called as refresher course.

Regarding the orientation training, all the respondents attended for 3 months, except 14% of the respondents of Srikalahasthi, who told that they have attended 4 months training progrmme.

Apart from the orientation training, all the respondents attended the refresher training for a week to a month. Some of them also attended these training programmes for more than once.

Table—4.83 Utility of the Training Programme

Utility	CGL	SKHT	PLNR	TPL	TPT	Total	%
Learned more about ICDS services	7	–	3	5	–	15	17.4
Learned about Immunization	2	5	4	2	2	15	17.4
Learned about how to mingle with community	3	6	–	1	1	11	12.8
Learned about how to conduct pre-school	3	5	–	–	–	8	9.3
Learned about preparation of teaching aids	–	3	–	–	4	7	8.1
Learned about health and nutrition	–	8	–	–	–	8	9.3
Learned about maintenance of registers	–	2	–	–	4	6	7.0
Learned about how to decrease the drop-outs	–	1	–	–	3	4	4.7
How to maintain AWC according to ICDS objectives	–	–	4	–	–	4	4.7
Learned about how to conduct meetings	–	–	–	2	–	2	2.3
Learned about non-formal education	–	–	2	–	–	2	2.3
Learned about family planning methods	–	2	–	–	–	2	2.3
Learned some songs	1	–	–	–	–	1	1.2
Sharing of experience	–	–	–	–	1	1	1.2

Table—4.84 Responsibilities of the AWW

Responsibilities	CGL	SKHT	PLNR	TPL	TPT	Total	%
Giving Immunization to pregnants and children 0–6 years	10	8	10	10	9	47	94
Conducting pre-school programme	8	10	10	10	9	47	94
Giving health and nutrition education	6	5	8	6	8	33	66
SNF distribution	6	9	1	10	3	29	58
Mahila mandal formation	2	–	5	5	–	12	24
Referral services	4	3	5	8	3	23	26
Making home visits	–	1	8	1	4	14	28
Conducting survey	–	2	–	–	3	5	10
Motivating women to undergo tubectomy	–	3	–	–	–	3	6
Maintenance of registers	–	1	–	–	2	3	6
Organising thrift programme	1	–	–	–	–	1	2
Distribution of folic acid tablets	–	–	–	–	1	1	2
Health check-up to children	–	–	–	–	1	1	2

Fig. 4.17: Responsibilities of the AWW

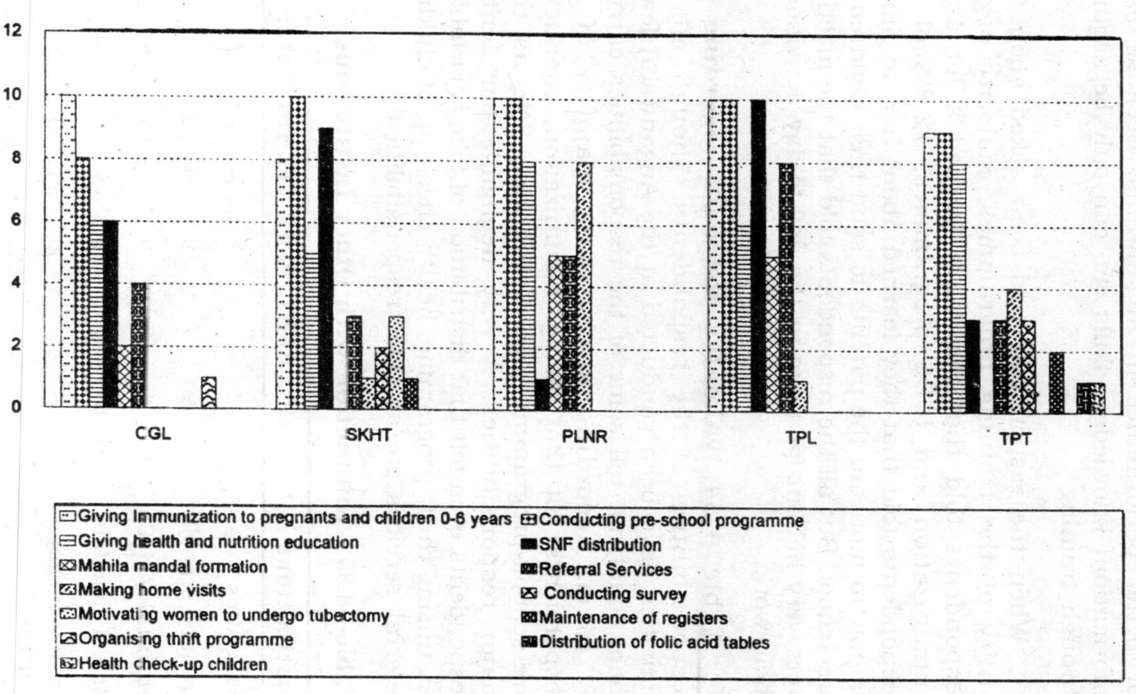

It is felt that respondents should be given training for better performance in Anganwadis. Because basic information, knowledge, skills etc. can only be acquired through training.

When the respondents had been asked about the utility of the training programmes, majority of the respondents told that they have learned a lot about Immunization and ICDS programmes, 12.8% of the respondents told that they learned about how to mingle or how to motivate the parents to send their children for pre-school. But all the respondents told that the meetings were very helpful for them in the day-to-day activities of their work.

Table 4.84, validates the data regarding job responsibilities of the respondents. Though all the activities have been conducted at the Anganwadi, few of them could not tell some of the responsibilities carrieed by them. According to the data, majority of the respondents felt that giving immunization, conducting pre-school programme and distributing SNF as their major responsibilities. A very negligible per cent of respondents even felf that distribution of folic acid tablets, organising thrift programme, health check-up of children, referral services etc as their responsibilities.

Table—4.85 Interaction with Other Institutions

Institutions	CGL	SKHT	PLNR	TPL	TPT	Total	%
Balwadies	2	–	–	–	–	2	1.5
Primary schools	9	7	9	10	2	37	27.8
Hospitals/PHCs	8	7	9	7	7	38	28.6
Mahila mandals	10	7	10	9	7	43	32.3
Adult education centres	–	–	6	1	1	8	6.0
Educational Institutes	–	–	3	1	–	4	3.0
Nursery schools	–	–	–	–	1	1	0.8

Fig. 4.18: Interaction with Other Institutions

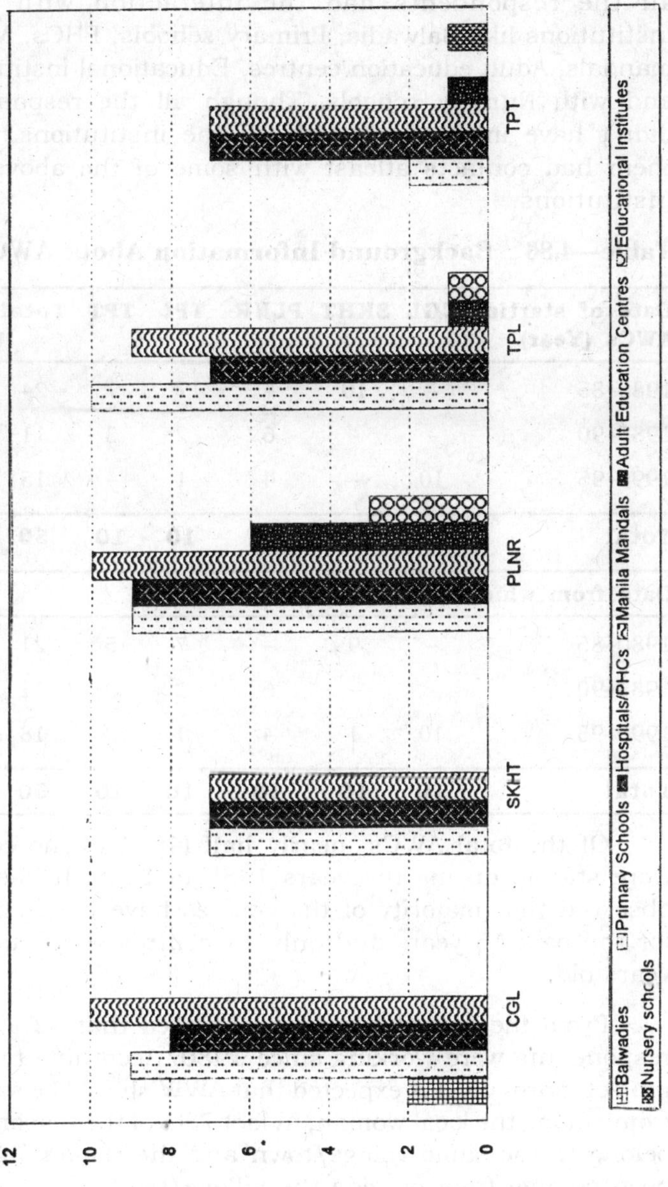

As ICDS is a multi-sectoral programme and involves several government and non-governmental organizations, all the respondents had the interaction with other institutions like Balwadis, Primary schools, PHCs, Mahila mandals, Adult education centres, Educational institutions and with Nursery schools. Though all the respondents didn't have interactions with all the institutions, all of them had contacts atleast with some of the above said institutions.

Table—4.86 Background Information About AWCs

Date of starting AWCs (Year)	CGL	SKHT	PLNR	TPL	TPT	Total	%
1980–85	–	10	–	7	7	24	48.0
1985–90	–	–	6	2	3	11	22.0
1990–95	10	–	4	1	–	15	30.0
Total	**10**	**10**	**10**	**10**	**10**	**50**	**100**
Date from which AWW is in position (Year)							
1980–85	–	9	–	7	5	21	42
1985–90	–	–	6	2	3	11	22
1990–95	10	1	4	1	2	18	36
Total	**10**	**10**	**10**	**10**	**10**	**50**	**100**

Of the total AWCs, nearly half (48%) of the centres were started during the years 1980 to 1985. It has been observed that majority of the centres have been running for the past 15 years and only 14 centres were just four years old.

From the data it has been observed that 42% of the respondents were working since 1980. According to ICDS project, normally it is expected that AWW should be selected from among the local woman, in fact 78% of the respondents belong to the same village/town and the remaining have been coming from outside the village/town.

Physical Infrastructure

According to ICDS project, local community should provide accommodation for AWC at free of cost. But in the study 80% of the centres were running in rented buildings by paying a rent of Rs. 50 to Rs. 150/- per month. It was also observed that, of the 10 centres, 7 had been constructed by the Government in Srikalahasthi project. But in Tirupati project, 9 centres were functioning in rented building, with a rent of Rs. 150/- per month.

Table—4.87 Details About the Space

Details	CGL	SKHT	PLNR	TPL	TPT	Total	%
Indoor space							
Adequate	5	9	4	3	8	29	58
Inadequate	5	1	6	7	2	21	42
Total	**10**	**10**	**10**	**10**	**10**	**50**	**100**
Outdoor space							
Adequate	7	10	6	8	7	38	76
Inadequate	3	–	4	2	3	12	24
Total	**10**	**10**	**10**	**10**	**10**	**50**	**100**

More than half of the centres had adequate indoor space as well as outdoor space. Only 24% of the respondents especially from Thamballapalli and Palamaneru projects told that outdoor space is inadequate for them.

Usage of toilets in rural areas particularly among the low-socio economic groups is quite uncommon. Hence in the present study, toilets were not available in 78% of the AWCs as the buildings belonged to them. Though toilet was available in the remaining centres, they were not utilised properly.

It was also observed that none of the centres were having separate cooking space, except two centres in Thamballapalle and one centre in Chinnagottugallu projects, because there was no need to cook as RTE (Ready to eat) food is available. With regard to the store room, about three-fourths of the centres were not having separate room to store things. But in Srikalahasthi, out of 10 centres, store room was available at 9 centres.

Table—4.88 Source of Drinking Water

Source	CGL	SKHT	PLNR	TPL	TPT	Total	%
Hand pump	8	8	9	8	3	36	72
Tap	2	1	–	2	7	12	24
Deep well	–	1	1	–	–	2	4
Total	**10**	**10**	**10**	**10**	**10**	**50**	**100**

Data related to sources of drinking water is presented in Table 4.88. Hand pump appeared to be the main source for majority of the centres. About one-fourths of the centres have public tap facility, and for the remaining centres deep well was the source.

Observations revealed that only charts, and some toys were available in majority of the centres. Most of the respondents of Srikalahasthi felt that they had not been given proper teaching aids except charts so they themselves prepared the articles by using clay, colour papers etc (Table 4.89).

According to Table 4.90, only plates and glasses were there in almost all the centres. Nearly half of the AWCs have bucket, wooden box, laddle, water container and medical kit. The below were the remaining equipment. available in AWCs.

The success of any welfare programme depends on the support and co-operation received from the community (Table 4.91). The implementation of the ICDS scheme, it is hoped, will eventually be taken over by the

Table—4.89 Teaching Aids Available in AWCs

Teaching aids	CGL	SKHT	PLNR	TPL	TPT	Total	%
Charts	7	10	10	9	7	43	86.0
Puppets	7	–	6	9	–	22	44.0
Toys	9	5	6	5	8	33	66.0
Blackboard	6	–	7	10	–	23	46.0
Flash cards	2	7	–	3	7	19	38.0
Colour pencils	1	–	3	–	–	4	8.0
Story books	–	–	7	–	–	7	14.0
Beeds	–	1	–	–	–	1	2.0
Self made articles	–	10	–	–	6	16	32.0
Picture books	–	–	–	2	–	2	4.0

Table—4.90 Equipment in the AWCs

Equipment	CGL	SKHT	PLNR	TPL	TPT	Total	%
Plates and glasses	8	10	10	10	8	46	92.0
Weighing machine	–	10	–	–	7	17	34.0
Wooden box	–	10	6	3	4	23	46.0
Medical kit	–	10	–	–	10	20	40.0
Drum	–	10	–	–	2	12	24.0
Desk	–	8	–	–	–	8	16.0
Basin	–	10	1	1	3	15	30.0
Laddles	–	10	1	2	10	23	46.0
Water container	7	10	6	–	2	25	50.0
Jug	1	10	–	4	2	17	34.0
Chairs	1	3	–	1	9	14	28.0
Table	–	2	–		2	4	8.0
Almairah (Iron)	–	–	3	2	7	12	24.0
Bucket	6	–	10	9	2	27	54.0
Mirror	1	–	–	–	–	1	2.0
Tub	1	–	–	–	–	1	2.0
Vessels	–	–	6	1	–	7	14.0

community. The scheme has a built-in mechanism of involving the community. In the study 72% of the respondents told that they had co-operation from the community. In majority of the cases, the community was providing only assistance in the form of labour.

Table—4.91 Community Participation

Participation	CGL	SKHT	PLNR	TPL	TPT	Total	%
Cash	–	1	–	–	5	6	10.3
Labour	4	9	7	3	5	28	48.3
Material	–	4	–	–	4	8	13.8
Nil	6	–	3	7	–	16	27.6

The data in Table 4.92 shows that the number of beneficiaries enrolled for the SNF, and those, who actually received the benefit. Up to 75 children were enrolled among the children of 6 months to 3 years of age. Ten to thirty one children were enrolled in 70% of the centres. When looked into the number actually receiving SNF, out of 75 children around 50 children were receiving SNF daily.

Table—4.92 Details Regarding SNF

	Total Number Enrolled						
No. of beneficiaries	**CGL**	**SKHT**	**PLNR**	**TPL**	**TPT**	**Total**	**%**
6 months to 3 years children.							
< 10	–	–	–	–	2	2	4
10–20	6	–	6	2	8	22	44
21–31	3	5	2	3	–	13	26
32–42	–	3	1	5	–	9	18
43–53	–	1	–	–	–	1	2
54–64	1	1	–	–	–	2	4
65–75	–	–	1	–	–	1	2
Total	**10**	**10**	**10**	**10**	**10**	**50**	**100**

(Contd...)

Pregnant							
5–10	4	1	3	5	7	20	40
11–16	2	4	4	5	1	16	32
17–22	4	3	1	–	1	9	18
23–28	–	2	2	–	1	5	10
Total	**10**	**10**	**10**	**10**	**10**	**50**	**100**
Malnourished							
Nil	8	6	8	6	4	32	64
1–2	2	4	2	4	6	18	36
Total	**10**	**10**	**10**	**10**	**10**	**50**	**100**
6m—6y Children							
30–40	2	–	1	1	1	5	10
41–51	4	1	5	3	5	18	36
52–62	3	3	3	2	3	14	28
63–73	–	3	1	3	–	7	14
74–85	–	1	–	1	1	3	6
86–96	–	1	–	–	–	1	2
97–107	1	1	–	–	–	2	4
Total	**10**	**10**	**10**	**10**	**10**	**50**	**100**

	Number Actually Receiving						
No. of beneficiaries	**CGL**	**SKHT**	**PLNR**	**TPL**	**TPT**	**Total**	**%**
< 10	–	–	–	–	2	2	4
10–20	6	1	6	3	8	24	48
21–31	3	7	4	3	–	17	34
32–42	–	2	–	4	–	6	12
43–53	1	–	–	–	–	1	2
54–64	–	–	–	–	–	–	–
65–75	–	–	–	–	–	–	–
Total	**10**	**10**	**10**	**10**	**10**	**50**	**100**

(Contd...)

Pregnant							
5–10	4	2	4	5	8	23	46
11–16	2	4	5	5	1	17	34
17–22	4	3	1	–	1	9	18
23–28	–	1	–	–	–	1	2
Total	**10**	**10**	**10**	**10**	**10**	**50**	**100**
Malnourished							
Nil	–	–	–	–	–	–	–
1–2	2	4	2	3	6	18	36
Total	–	–	–	–	–	–	–
6m—6y Children							
30–40	4	–	3	3	5	15	30
41–51	2	4	4	2	4	16	32
52–62	3	5	3	2	1	14	28
63–73	–	1	–	3	–	4	8
74–85	–	–	–	–	–	–	–
86–96	1	–	–	–	–	1	2
97–107	–	–	–	–	–	–	–
Total	**10**	**10**	**10**	**10**	**10**	**50**	**100**

In 6 months to 6 year children category, 30 to 73 children were enrolled in majority (88%) of the centres. Except 10% of AWCs, only 30 to 62 children were actually coming for SNF.

It is happy to note that there were no malnourished children in 64% of the centres. Even in the remaining 36% of the centres, only one or two children were enrolled and all the malnourished children were getting SNF daily.

Among pregnant and lactating mothers category 5 to 28 beneficiaries had been registered from each centre. Almost all the enrolled beneficiaries were coming for SNF.

Table 4.93 helps in understanding the number of children enrolled for pre-school education by AWW, and the number of children coming regularly to AWC in each project. It has been noticed that 15 to 55 children were enrolled in each AWC for pre-school education but more than 38 children were not attending in any centre. Only 15 to 38 children were attending in all the centres, because, the respondents told that most of the parents were interested to send their children to convents instead of sending to AWC.

Table—4.93 Details Regarding Pre-school Education

Pre-school education	CGL	SKHT	PLNR	TPL	TPT	Total	%
Total Number Enrolled							
15–20	2	1	–	2	–	5	10
21–26	3	7	1	3	–	14	28
27–32	3	2	5	4	3	17	34
33–38	2	1	–	1	1	4	8
39–44	–	–	3	–	6	9	18
45–55	–	–	1	–	–	1	2
Total	**10**	**10**	**10**	**10**	**10**	**50**	**100**
Number Actually Receiving							
15–20	4	4	1	5	–	14	28
21–26	2	6	5	2	–	15	30
27–32	4	–	2	3	5	14	28
33–38	–	–	2	–	5	7	14
39–44	–	–	–	–	–	–	–
45–55	–	–	–	–	–	–	–
Total	**10**	**10**	**10**	**10**	**10**	**50**	**100**

The common activities for pre-school education followed by all AWWs were prayer, health check-up, aksharagnanam (knowledge of alphabets), story telling, feeding, indoor/outdoor games, creative activities, which lead to the total development of the child.

Table—4.94 Details of Health Check-up Given to Pregnant Women

No. of Pregnants	CGL	SKHT	PLNR	TPL	TPT	Total	%
1–2	2	1	–	–	2	5	10
3–4	3	4	3	3	5	18	36
5–6	1	–	3	5	2	11	22
7–8	3	1	2	1	–	7	14
9–10	1	–	2	–	1	4	8
Nil	–	4	–	1	–	5	10
Total	**10**	**10**	**10**	**10**	**10**	**50**	**100**

The medical and para-medical personnel visited the AWCs periodically. Hence pregnant women could take the opportunity for seeking advise from the medical and para-medical personnel visiting AWC. From the data it has been noted that except in 5 AWCs, one to ten pregnant women from each centre have utilized this service. With regard to the children's health check-up, the AWWs only make sure that their clothes are clean, hair properly combed and nails regularly cut etc.

Immunization Given to Children

According to majority of the respondents, the health personnel have not given much importance to booster dose (DT) which has to be given at the age of 5 years. But Polio and DPT vaccinations were given promptly to the children who were in appropriate age to get these vaccinations.

Vaccination Against TT to Pregnant Women

Enquiries revealed that all the pregnant women in every AWC of each project were vaccinated against Tetanus Toxoid. Hence it indicates that ICDS has been relatively successful in reaching the certain groups even in the far flung and isolated areas.

AWW has the responsibility in creating awareness on health and nutrition among pregnant, lactating and mothers of pre-school children. Charts, books, black board, puppets, picture cards etc. were the teaching aids used by the AWWs of Chinnagottigallu, Palamaneru, and Thamballa palle projects. All the AWWs of Srikalahasthi, and Tirupati, told that they were using the methods of both discussion and demonstration to impart the knowledge about health and nutrition.

Table—4.95 Details of Health and Nutrition Education

Health and Nutrition Education	CGL	SKHT	PLNR	TPL	TPT	Total	%
(a) Educational Methods							
Discussion and Demonstration	–	10	–	–	10	20	27.0
Charts	4	–	8	8	–	20	27.0
Books	–	–	3	–	–	3	4.1
Black board	4	–	3	6	–	13	17.6
Group discussion	–	–	2	–	–	2	2.7
Puppets	2	–	1	8	–	11	14.9
Picture cards	–	–	–	5	–	5	6.7

(Contd...)

(b) Topics Discussed							
Importance of Greens/ SNF/Ragi etc.	9	6	10	8	5	38	37.6
Cleanliness and personal hygiene	7	3	1	–	5	16	15.8
Immunization	–	–	–	–	5	5	5.0
Root causes for different diseases	–	–	–	–	3	3	2.9
Preparation of ORS	–	9	–	–	2	11	11.0
Weaning foods	–	1	–	1	2	4	4.0
Family planning	–	1	–	–	2	3	2.9
Foods to be taken during pregnancy	7	3	–	3	5	18	17.8
Children nutritive foods	–	–	–	1	–	1	1.0
Importance of breast feeding	–	1	–	1	–	2	2.0
(c) Time							
10–11 AM	8	–	–	–	–	8	16
2–4 PM	2	–	10	7	–	19	38
5–6 PM	–	–	–	2	–	2	4
During SNF distribution	–	2	–	–	3	5	10
During home visits	–	3	–	–	2	5	10
Monthly once at any convenient time	–	5	–	1	5	11	22

As most of the women neglect the green leafy vegetables, which is easily available and which is rich in Vitamin A, Iron and Calcium. Majority of the AWWs disccussed about the importance of greens, ragi and also the SNF which will be given at AWC. Foods to be taken during pregnancy, cleanliness, personal hygiene, preparation and utilization of ORS etc. were the common topics discussed by relatively higher per cent of respondents.

In general, monthly once the AWW had meetings with mothers and pregnant women. During that time the AWWs had the discussions on various topics. But 20% of the respondents told that they were informed at the time of SNF distribution and during home visits about the health and nutrition.

Table—4.96 Objectives—Told by AWWs

Objectives	CGL	SKHT	PLNR	TPL	TPT	Total	%
Immunization to 0–6 year children & pregnant women	10	7	10	7	7	41	24.6
Health & nutrition education to mother	8	4	10	7	6	35	21.0
Pre-school education	8	4	10	9	4	35	21.0
Physical & mental development of children	–	3	–	–	5	8	4.8
Pre-natal/post-natal services	–	3	–	–	–	3	1.8
Referral services	5	–	10	7	–	22	13.2
Distribution of SNF	7	–	–	8	–	15	9.0
Reduction of IMR	–	2	–	–	3	5	3.0
Women & Child welfare services	–	2	–	–	–	2	1.1
Home Visits	–	–	1	–	–	1	0.5

The data depicted in Table 4.96 tells that objectives of the ICDS as expressed by the respondents. It was surprising to note that no respondent could tell all the objectives. Some of them could tell by mixing objectives and services. Majority of them could tell about the

Fig. 4.19: Objectives—Told by AWWs

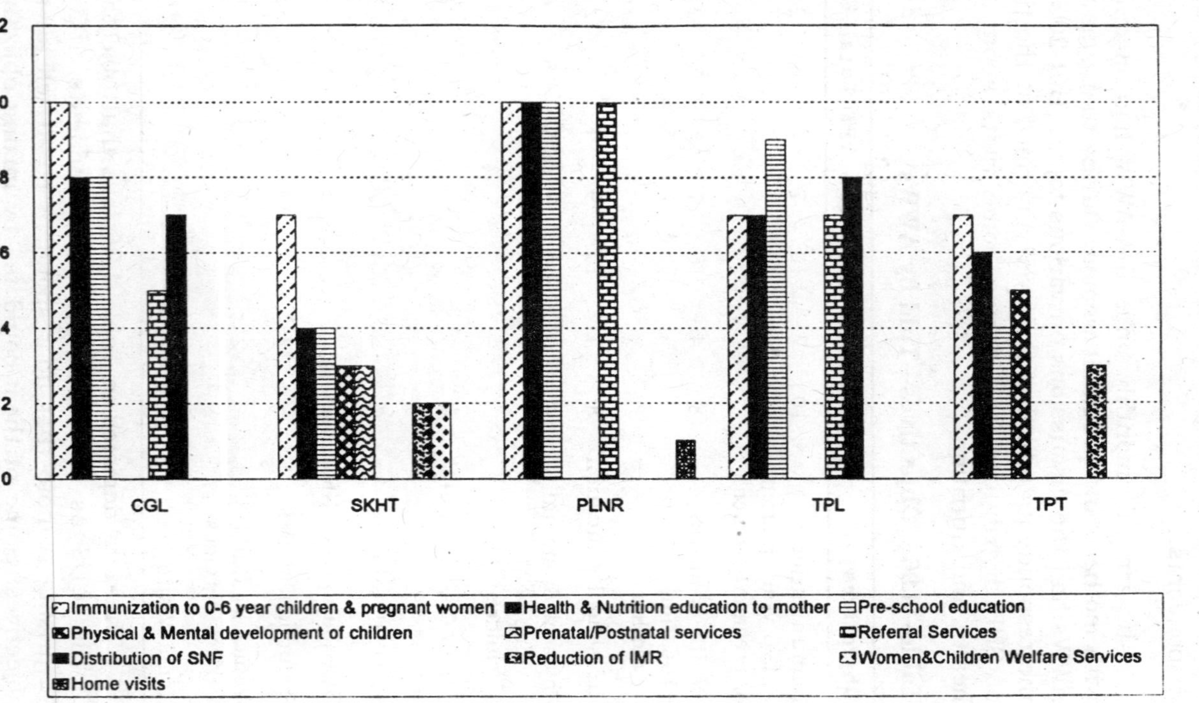

immunization which is to be given to 0-6 year children and pregnant women. Hence it is necessary that AWWs should be equipped with sufficient knowledge about the objectives of ICDS. The reason could be the AWWs may not have been trained properly or techniques adopted for training might not be appropriate for them.

Table—4.97 Main Activities of AWCs

Activities	CGL	SKHT	PLNR	TPL	TPT	Total	%
Conducting pre-school	8	10	10	9	10	47	94.8
Distribution of SNF	10	10	10	8	10	48	96.0
Giving Immunization	9	10	10	7	10	46	92.0
Giving Health and nutrition education	6	8	10	7	10	41	82.0
Making home visits	4	1	5	6	10	27	54.0
Referral services	3	1	10	7	2	23	46.0
Medical help	–	–	–	–	3	3	6.0
Organising thrift programme	6	–	–	–	–	6	12.0
Conducting meetings	–	–	2	–	–	2	4.0

AWW has to perform several tasks at AWC. When asked to tell the main activities of their centres, more than 90% of the beneficiaries told that conducting pre-school, distribution of SNF and providing Immunization to children and pregnant women were their main activities. 54% of the respondents could tell that making home-visits as their main activity which is very important to identify pre-school children, pregnant women and lactating mothers. Though all the respondents were doing all the activities which were mentioned in Table 4.97, only few of them could tell about referral services, organising thrift programmes, extending medical help, conducting meetings etc. The reason could be that they were not showing proper interest on these activities.

Fig. 4.20: Main Activities of AWCs

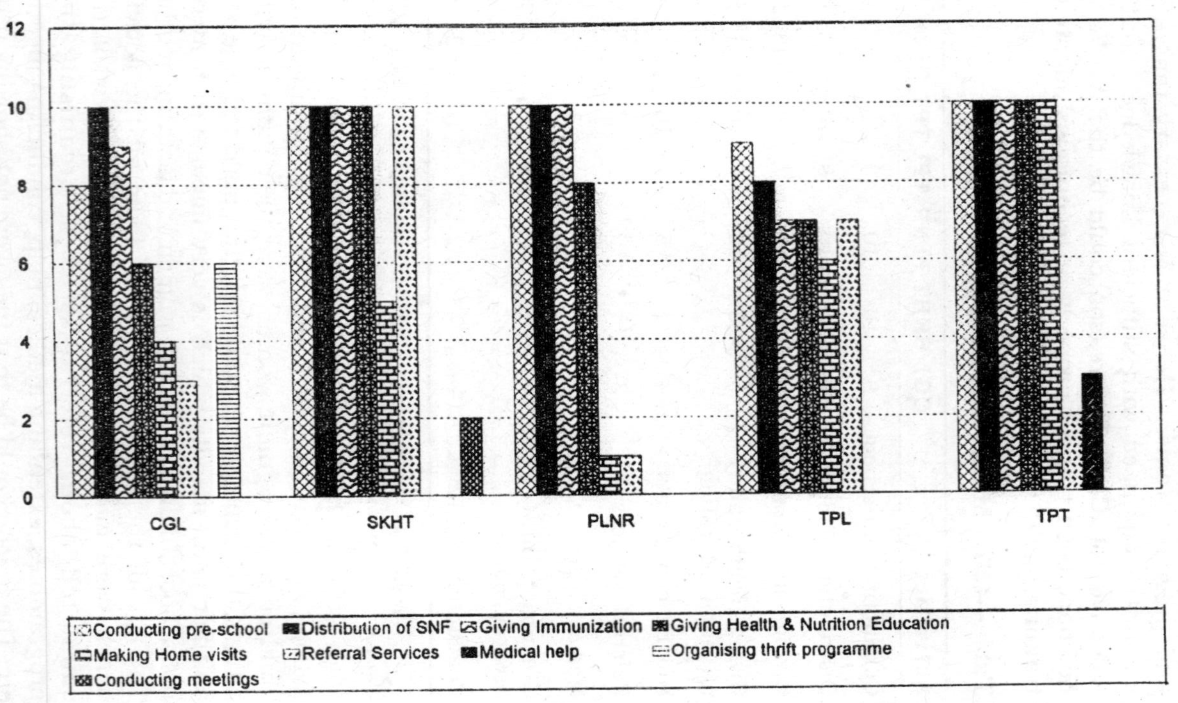

Criteria Followed in Selecting the Beneficiaries

As per the rules, beneficiaries should be selected based on their caste, family size, health and nutritional status, income level etc. But in practice, all the respondents told that they were enrolling all the children between 0-6 years of age, pregnant women and lactating mothers, those who have evinced interest towards the benefits of AWC, irrespective of their income, caste, family size etc.

Table—4.98 Registers Maintaining by AWWs

Registers	CGL	SKHT	PLNR	TPL	TPT	Total	%
Staff attendance register	10	10	10	10	10	50	100
Immunization register	10	10	10	10	10	50	100
Feeding register	10	10	10	10	10	50	100
Survey register	10	10	10	10	10	50	100
Pre-school attendance register	10	10	10	10	10	50	100
Food stock register	10	10	10	10	10	50	100
Visitors register	10	10	–	10	10	40	80
Mothers meeting register	10	–	10	10	10	40	80
Pregnant women and lactating mothers register	10	–	–	10	10	30	60
Growth chart register	10	10	–	–	10	30	60
Home visits register	–	–	10	10	10	30	60
Birth and death register	10	10	–	–	10	30	60
Referral services register	10	10	–	–	10	30	60
Diary	10	–	10	–	10	30	60
Permanent assets register	10	10	–	–	10	30	60
Mahila mandal register	–	10	10	10	–	30	60
Monthly progress report register	–	10	10	10	–	30	60

(Contd...)

Medical stock register	–	10	–	–	10	20	40
3rd & 4th grade children register	–	10	–	–	10	20	40
Consumable assets register	–	10	–	–	10	20	40
Survey abstract register	–	–	–	–	10	10	20
0—1 year children register	–	–	–	–	10	10	20
0-6 year children register	–	–	–	–	10	10	20
Out patients register	–	–	–	–	10	10	20
Medicine issues register	–	10	–	–	–	10	20
Family planning	–	–	10	–	–	10	20
Thrift programme register	–	–	–	10	–	10	20

Maintenance of registers is also one of the primary duties of the AWWs. They told that all the AWWs of each project have to maintain the same registers. According to the instructions given by CDPO, AWWs were maintaining the register. It has been noted that staff attendance register, immunization register and feeding register etc were the registers, which had been maintained by all the AWWs in all the projects.

As AWWs have to perform several tasks, they might have problems also. In order to understand their problems, data was collected with regard to problems faced by the respondents. Table 4.99 revealed that only 40% of the respondents had no problems in the implementation of the programme. Of the remaining, irregular supply of SNF and lack of toys to play for the children etc., were the problems for majority of the respondents. Lack of proper buildings to maintain AWC is also one of the problem expressed by 7.4% of the respondents. More than half of the respondents of Thamballapalli told that they were not getting honorarium and TA & DA properly. Another interesting problem expressed was that 3% of the respondents from Tirupati project told that they were being called as a worker only, though they educate women and children. They felt that they don't want to be

Table—4.99 Problems Encountered in the Implementation of ICDS

Problems	CGL	SKHT	PLNR	TPL	TPT	Total	%
Lack of adequate toys to children	–	6	–	–	–	6	8.8
Lack of proper building for AWC	–	3	–	–	2	5	7.4
Maintenance of registers is difficult	–	3	–	–	–	3	4.4
Booster doses (DT) are not giving properly	–	2	–	–	–	2	2.9
Superstitious believes are more in the area	–	1	–	–	–	1	1.5
Motivation was difficult	–	1	–	–	2	3	4.4
Looking down by the community as we receive lower remuneration	–	1	–	–	–	1	1.5
Distribution of SNF is difficult as non beneficiaries also comes during distribution	1	–	–	–	–	1	1.5
Not getting honararium regularly	–	–	–	2	–	2	2.9
Not getting TA & DA properly	–	–	–	4	–	4	5.9
Irregularity in supplying SNF	4	–	–	2	–	6	8.8
Getting very less remuneration	–	–	–	2	–	2	2.9
Lack of proper visits by supervisors	–	–	–	1	–	1	1.5
School drop-outs were increasing day by day	–	–	–	–	1	1	1.5
Though we educate children & mothers, still we were being called as Worker	–	–	–	–	2	2	2.9
Lack of proper teaching aids	1	–	–	–	–	1	1.5
No problems	5	3	10	4	5	27	39.7

Fig. 4.21: Problems Encountered in the Implementation of ICDS

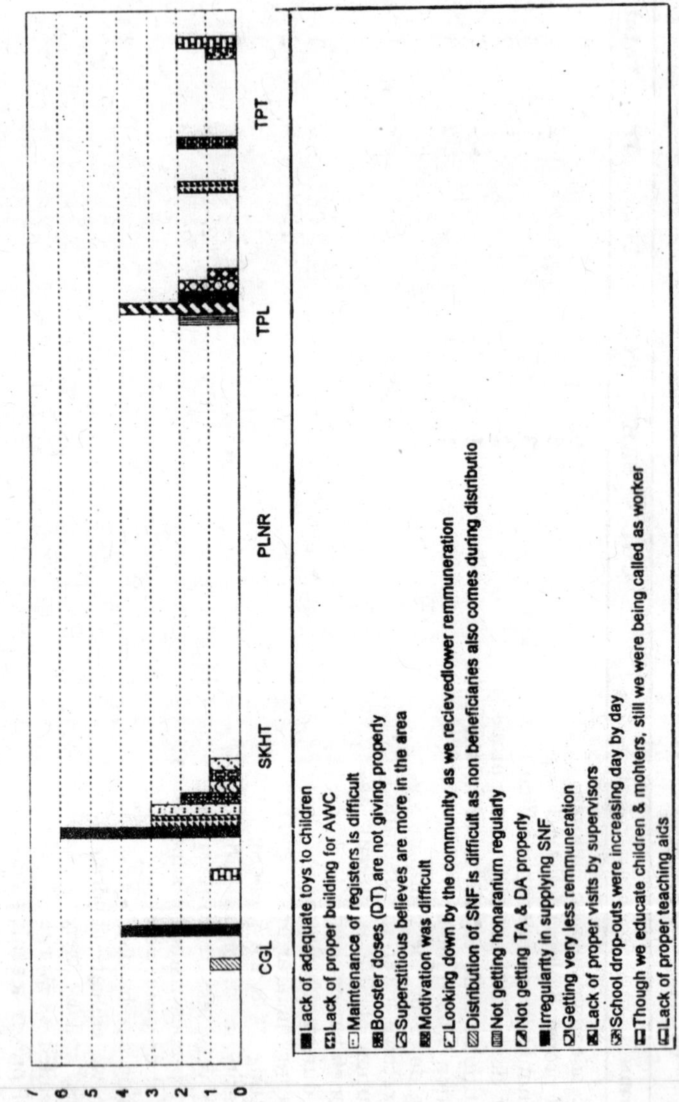

called as worker. Though they were facing different problems in the implementation, 100% of the respondents told that this programme has met some of the needs of the people from villages.

Table—4.100 Kind of Needs Solved

Needs	CGL	SKHT	PLNR	TPL	TPT	Total	%
Immunization	10	6	10	7	8	41	29.2
Pre-school	5	8	9	7	4	33	23.4
Relief from starvation	8	5	7	5	4	29	20.6
Health & Nutrition Education	–	–	7	3	5	15	10.6
Availability of medical help	–	8	–	–	1	9	6.4
Mothers were going to work by leaving their child at AWC	–	5	–	–	–	5	3.5
Referral services	–	–	2	3	–	5	3.5
Thrift programme	4		–	–	–	4	2.8

Details regarding the problems solved through ICDS have been presented in Table 4.100. ICDS programme is seen as major innovative effort in building comprehensive integrated services for mother and children. Health and nutrition services, being important components of the ICDS scheme, 73% of the respondents told that, when there was no AWC, their villagers were unaware of vaccinations. Getting the benefit of immunization at their door steps, pre-school education, SNF etc appeared to be the main advantages of the scheme for the people in their villages. According to more than half of the respondents of Srikalahasthi project, availability of medical help is a boon for their local community. On the whole all the respondents felt that the life styles of their people have been changed through the scheme.

Table—4.101 Achievements Through the Scheme

Achievements	CGL	SKHT	PLNR	TPL	TPT	Total	%
Coming forward for immunization	6	6	8	4	5	29	34.5
Keeping their surroundings clean	–	5	–	–	3	8	9.5
Observed reduction in morbidity rate	–	5	–	–	3	8	9.5
Change is observed in cooking & food habits	2	5	7	3	1	18	21.4
Accepting tubectomy	–	–	–	–	1	1	1.2
Consuming SNF regularly	8	3	–	2	–	13	15.5
Utilising health services	2	–	–	1	–	3	3.6
Utilizing ICDS services	–	–	4	–	–	4	4.8

It is quite well-known that India is one of the countries where infant mortality, child mortality and maternal mortality rates are relatively high compared to other industrialised countries. The child health is especially dependent on mothers own well being and therefore, mother and child health have to be dealt with in an integrated manner which is one of the things that programmes like the ICDS try to ensure. It is evident from the fact that 100 per cent of the respondents told that ICDS scheme has improved the health and nutritional status of the women and children in their village. According to data depicted in table 101, 34.5% of the respondents told that their village women and children's health has improved because they were coming forward to get vaccinations without fear and hesitation. Another 21.4% told that change has been observed in their cooking practices and also in the food habits too. Due to regular consumption of SNF which is given at

Fig. 4.22: Achievements Through the Scheme

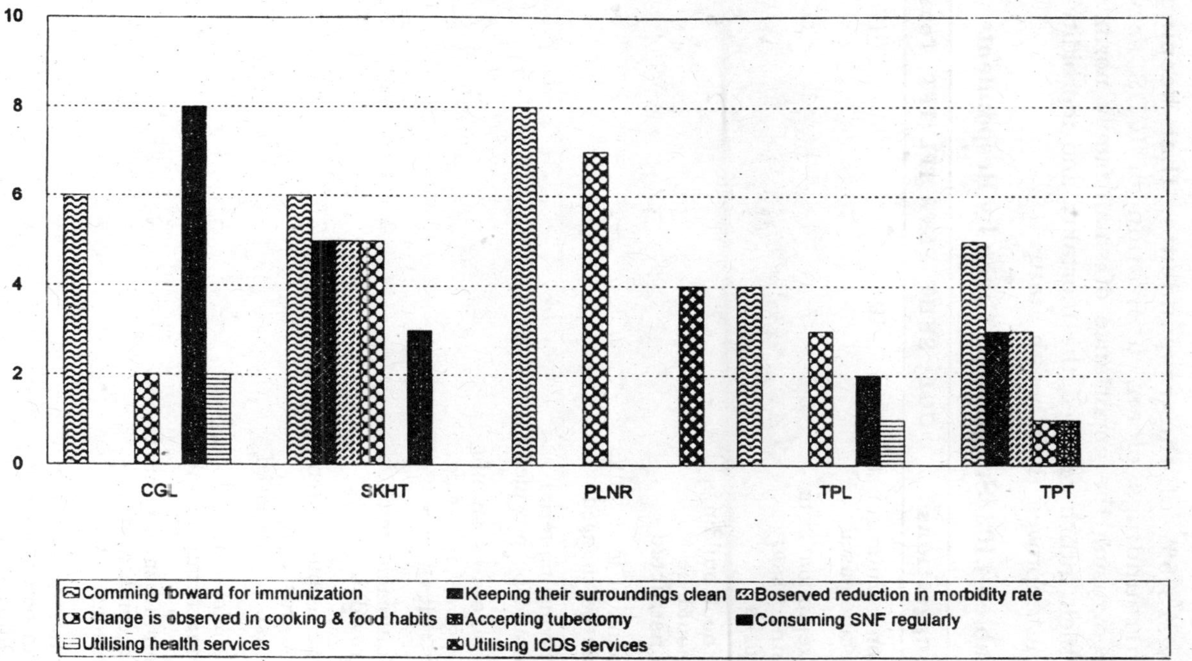

AWC, their health has been improved. It has been stated by 15.5% of the respondents, that keeping the surroundings clean, utilization of ICDS. services, recognising the importance of small family norm, all of which inturn reduced the mortality and morbidity rates and improved their health status.

Table—4.102 Suggestions Given by Respondents

Suggestions	CGL	SKHT	PLNR	TPL	TPT	Total	%
Honararium must be increased	–	10	–	–	7	17	24.0
Exemption from unnecessary works	3	7	4	–	3	17	24.0
School buildings should be constructed	–	2	1	–	2	5	7.1
Items of food stuffs can be changed	–	3	–	–	2	5	7.1
Playing material should be provided	–	6	–	–	–	6	8.5
Promotions should be given according to rules	–	2	–	–	–	2	2.8
Equipment must be provided	–	–	2	–	–	2	2.8
The amount given towards rent must be increased	–	–	2	–	–	2	2.8
Officials should concentrate on AWC	–	–	–	2	–	2	2.8
Immunization must be conducted through AWC	–	–	–	2	–	2	2.8
Summer vacation can be given to children	–	–	–	–	1	1	1.4

(Contd...)

SNF (powder) can be replaced by rice	–	–	1	–	–	1	1.4
Supply of SNF should be regularised	1	–	–	–	–	1	1.4
Everybody should work sincerely	–	–	–	1	–	1	1.4
In thrift programme, loan can be given upto Rs. 5000/-	–	–	–	1	–	1	1.4
No suggestions	9	–	4	4	–	17	23.9

Table 4.102 is drawn based on the suggestions given by respondents for better implementation of the programme. Over discussion, most (24%) of the respondents (all the respondents of SKHT) suggested that their honorarium should be increased, as it is difficult to meet their needs with the very small amount which they are getting now. They opined that if they were given good amount of salary, they said that they could concentrate better and for more on work. Since there were no play materials at AWCs, 8.5% of them suggested that play material should be provided which is very important to attract the children. Seven per cent of them told that school dropouts can be prevented by offering different types of eatables, instead of giving same type of powdered food (weaning food) daily, and some of them felt that the promotions should be given for eligible AWWs by considering the rules and regulations. To work effectively AWWs need further encouragement. One third of the respondents didn't give any suggestions. The above stated suggestions had also been given by the remaining respondents.

All the respondents are of the same opinion that CDPO should monitor the centre regularly for effective implementation of the programme. (1.103) At present there is no CDPO in Tirupati project, hence Medical

Fig. 4.23: Suggestions Given by Respondents

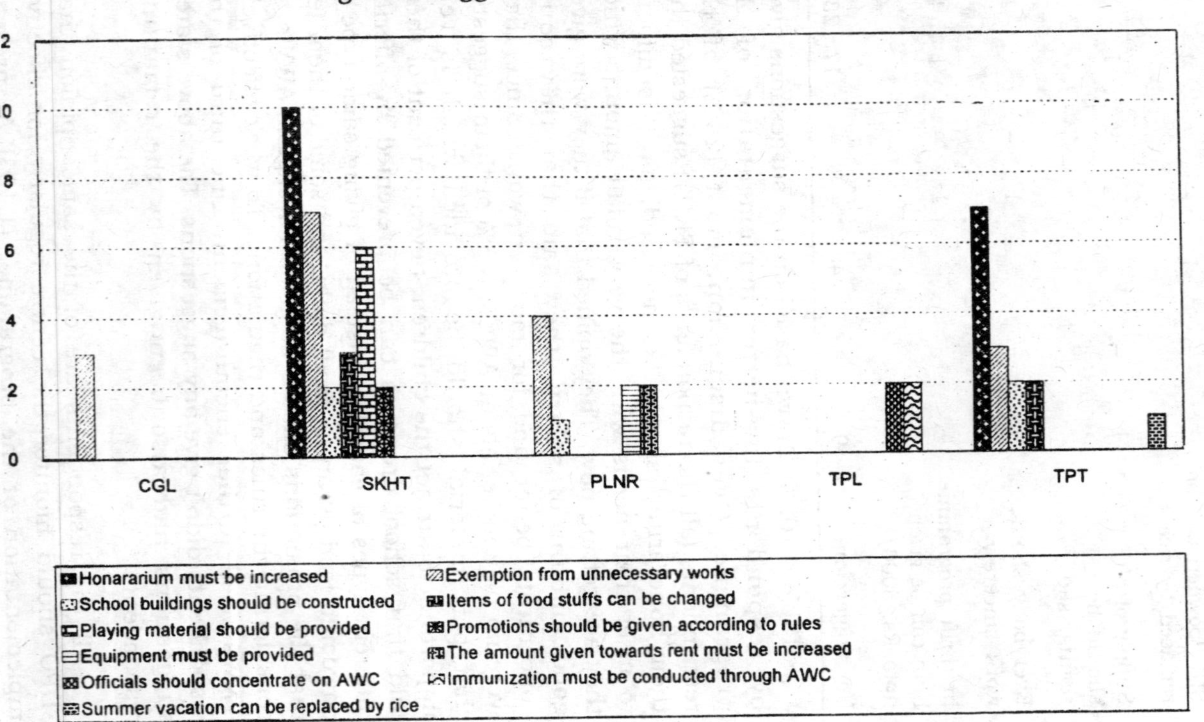

Officer is fulfilling the responsibilities of CDPO. 40% of the respondents told that, their CDPO/Medical Officer visits their centres once in a month. The remaining visited occasionally. But supervisors visited all the centres monthly once, even twice in Palamaneru project.

Table—4.103 Frequency of Visits by Officials

Officials	CGL	SKHT	PLNR	TPL	TPT	Total	%
CDPO/Medical Officer							
Once in a month	–	–	10	–	10	20	40
Occasionally	10	10	–	10	–	30	60
Supervisor							
Once in a month	10	10	–	10	10	40	80
Twice in a month	–	–	10	–	–	10	.20

100% of the respondents told that the supervisor checks and gives suggestions in maintenance of registers. Where as CDPO/Medical officer checks all the activities of AWC and inspects the children by enquiring and gives suggestions for improvement of the activities of the centre. All the respondents told that monthly reports will be checked at CDPO's office every month. CDPO and supervisors checks the reports by comparing them with previous monthly reports. If they find any mistakes, they often seek explanation for the mistakes.

Participation of Non-officials

Except one or two centres of Srikalahasti and Tirupati projects, non ICDS officials like Panchayat leaders, Mahila mandal Presidents, School teachers were also involving themselves in the activities of AWC and extending their full support when ever the respondents were in need.

According to Table 4.104 most of the (30.9%) respondents had given importance to availability of space which is very essential for the children to play, followed by 28% who had considered the availability of safe drinking water as a primary issue in locating the AWC.

Table—4.104 Criteria in Locating AWC

Criteria	CGL	SKHT	PLNR	TPL	TPT	Total	%
Availability of sufficient space	6	2	10	10	5	33	30.9
Availability of safe drinking water	10	–	10	5	5	30	28.0
Accessibility	5	–	7	5	5	22	20.6
Availability of building	–	10	–	–	4	14	13.1
Population	–	3	–	–	1	4	3.7
Co-operation	–	3	–	–	1	4	3.7

As it is very difficult to get a house to run Anganwadi Centre with meagre amount of rent with all facilities, all the respondents of Srikalahasti project, told that their first preference has been to get a building even if it does not have all the facilities. Accessibility, population and co-operation etc were also the criteria followed in locating AWC.

Table—4.105 Equipment in AWC

Equipment	CGL	SKHT	PLNR	TPL	TPT	Total	%
Multipurpose items	3	3	3	9	7	25	50
Kitchen equipments	8	10	10	9	9	46	92
Bathroom equipments	7	4	10	9	5	35	70
Indoor play equipment	8	3	10	8	5	34	68
Outdoor play equipment	–	–	–	–	–	–	–

The Kitchen equipment, which included tumblers, plates and spoons, water drums, etc. were the only available equipment in almost all the AWCs followed by bathroom equipment like bucket or vessels for storing water, mugs etc which were available in 70% of the centres, outdoor play equipment was not available at any of the centres. The reason could be that several outdoor games can be conducted without any equipment and the requisite funds were also not available to procure play equipment.

The ICDS programme has scope for coverage of various welfare measures for the well being of mother and children in particular and community in general. It is only the AWW, the grass root level functionary whose responsibilities are many folded in the successful implementation of the programme. There is no doubt that AWW plays a crucial role in reaching all the package of services to the needy people.

PROFILE OF THE SUPERVISOR

The Anganwadi worker is in constant need for guidance and close supervision for ensuring that the objectives of the ICDS programme are achieved. As the AWW is with a rural background, from low income group and in general no education. Hence, regular supervision is provided by the supervisor to help her to solve the problems related to the functioning of AWC. The supervisor serves as a liaison between the CDPO and AWW. The job responsibilities of supervisors are, providing continuous guidance to AWW to bridge the gap between training and job requirements, visiting AWC at least once a month and giving guidance in conducting house surveys, enlisting of beneficiaries, identification of 'at risk' children and mothers, and checking the records and work of AWW. Organising monthly meetings with the participation concerned LHV and ANMs. Ensuring timely submission of monthly progress reports by AWWs to CDPO and checking the accuracy of these reports. Assisting the CDPO in payment of honoraria to AWW and Helper, finalising the convenient dates for monthly meetings, issue of materials to AWCs etc.

Apart from above said responsibilities the supervisor is expected to assist CDPOs in identifying place for location and/or for construction of AWCs. She has to supervise the installation of hand pumps and smokeless chulla's, sanitary latrines and water filters at AWCs, she has to guide AWWs those who are conducting NAEP, DWCRA scheme, she has to co-ordinate with extension staff, and guide the AWW in each and every aspect, for the welfare of the women and children.

Data had been collated from 23 supervisors and presented in Table 4.106 to 4.119.

Table—4.106 Age of the Respondents

Age in years	CGL	SKHT	PLNR	TPL	TPT	Total	%
15–20	–	–	–	–	1	1	4.3
25–30	–	–	–	–	–	–	–
30–35	1	1	1	1	3	7	30.4
35–40	1	2	3	3	–	9	39.2
40–45	1	–	–	–	1	2	8.7
45–50	1	1	2	–	–	4	17.4
Total	**4**	**4**	**6**	**4**	**5**	**23**	**100**

The age profile of the respondents as indicated in Table 4.106 shows clearly that a more than two-thirds of them were between the age of 30-40 years. The percentage of respondents above 45 years and below 30 years was comparatively low. All of them were Hindus except one (4.5%) who is a Christian.

Table—4.107 Caste and Tribe of the Respondents

	CGL	SKHT	PLNR	TPL	TPT	Total	%
Farward Caste	3	2	4	3	3	15	65.3
Backward Caste	–	1	2	2	1	6	26.1
Scheduled Caste	1	–	–	–	–	1	4.3
Scheduled Tribe	–	1	–	–	–	1	4.3
Total	**4**	**4**	**6**	**5**	**4**	**23**	**100.0**

The perusal of the data given in the above table indicates that, though all the castes represented, Forward caste occupy a high position. Only 9% of the respondents were scheduled caste and scheduled Tribes.

Table—4.108 Marital Status

Marital status	CGL	SKHT	PLNR	TPL	TPT	Total	%
Unmarried	–	1	–	–	2	3	13.0
Married	4	2	6	5	2	19	82.7
Widow	–	1	–	–	–	1	4.3
Total	**4**	**4**	**6**	**5**	**4**	**23**	**100**

Marital status of the supervisors of the five projects according to the data collected for the study is indicated in the Table 4.108. It shows that only 13% of them were unmarried and the remaining 82.7%were married and one was a widow.

Table—4.109 Educational Qualifications of the Respondents

Level of education	CGL	SKHT	PLNR	TPL	TPT	Total	%
SSC/SSLC	3	1	1	3	–	8	34.8
Intermediate	1	–	3	–	–	4	17.4
Graduation	–	3	1	1	–	5	21.7
Post-graduation	–	–	1	1	4	6	26.1
Total	**4**	**4**	**6**	**5**	**4**	**23**	**100.0**

Data pertaining to educational levels of the respondents has been presented in Table 4.109. According to the data, majority of the respondents completed their SSC/SSLC followed by 21.7% who have completed their Graduation fairly large number of them (26%) have completed even their Post-graduation.

Table—4.110 Total Length of Service

Service in years	CGL	SKHT	PLNR	TPL	TPT	Total	%
1–5	4	2	1	4	–	11	47.8
5–10	–	2	3	–	3	8	34.8
10–15	–	–	2	1	1	4	17.4
Total	**4**	**4**	**6**	**5**	**4**	**23**	**100**

Table 4.110 gives the details regarding the total length of service of the respondents. As per the data, more than 50% of the respondents were working for 5 to 15 years and the remaining 47.8% of the respondents have below 5 years of experience.

Table—4.111 Mode of Recruitment

Mode	CGL	SKHT	PLNR	TPL	TPT	Total	%
Through promotion	4	2	1	4	–	11	47.8
APPSC recruitment	–	2	5	1	4	12	52.2
Total	**4**	**4**	**6**	**5**	**4**	**23**	**100.0**

According to the data relatively a high per cent of respondents were Grade I supervisors, who had been recruited by Andhra Pradesh Public Service commission and the remaining 47.8% became supervisors through promotion, who were earlier Anganwadi workers.

Table—4.112 Details Regarding Training Programmes Attended

Name of the training	CGL	SKHT	PLNR	TPL	TPT	Total	%
Orientation Course	4	2	6	5	3	20	87.0
Refresher Course	–	2	5	1	1	9	39.0

Of the total 23 respondents only 87% (20) of the respondents had undergone the orientation training, and the remaining were appointed recently. The duration of the training is 90 days for 6 respondents, 40 days for 8 respondent and 15 days for the remaining respondents. Regarding the Refresher training, only 39% have attended. The duration of the training was 10-15 days. Three respondents (one from Tirupati and 2 from SKHT) attended neither orientation nor refresher training.

Table—4.113 Utility of the Training

Utility	CGL	SKHT	PLNR	TPL	TPT	Total	%
Learned more about implementation	–	2	–	–	2	4	20
Learned more about responsibilities	4	–	5	4	1	14	70
Learned how to mingle with the community during field visit	–	–	1	1	–	2	10
Total	**4**	**2**	**6**	**5**	**3**	**20**	**100**

Of the total respondents who attended either training, majority of them told that they learned their responsibilities through such training. As equal number of respondents became supervisors from AWWs position. They didn't show their interest towards these training because of the feeling that they were well aware of the ICDS programmes.

Job Performance

When asked to tell their job-responsibilities as a supervisor almost all of them expressed identical views.They told that they were responsible in conducting immunization programme, by fixing a date with the consent of ANM and informing the date to AWW and make her to gather all the eligible children; giving guidance to

AWW in conducting pre-school. Regarding referral service, collecting all the 3rd and 4th grade children and mothers at risk, and refer them to PHCs regarding SNF, helping AWW in selecting beneficiaries, supervision of SNF were their responsibilities.

Regarding health check-up, extending help to ANM and AWW in conducting health check-up. Regarding nutrition and health education, to help the AWW, in conducting mothers meeting and in educating them in various aspects like importance of breast feeding, weaning foods, basic food groups, diseases due to nutritional deficiency, preventive measures etc. were their responsibilities. And they told that their job involves, checking records and registers, enthusing the AWW, community mobilization, on spot training to AWW, preparation of teaching aids, monitoring of AWW's work, and conducting mahila mandal meetings etc.

For the enquiry on when do they meet their superiors, all of them told that they went and met their CDPO/ACDPO on every Monday in the office and they told that the main objective of the ICDS was women and child welfare by providing the six packages of services. The main activities of their centres were running pre-school, distribution of SNF, conducting health and nutritional education and making the people to get immunization etc. The beneficiaries of the programme were children between 0-6 years, pregnant and lactating mothers and women of 15 to 45 years age based on their economic and social status.

The information regarding the records to be maintained by the supervisors is presented in Table 4.114. According to the data there is a difference between project to project in the maintenance of the records, but they are all maintaining not less than six different registers in every project.

According to the Table 4.115 data collected for the study, 39.1% told that they didn't come across any

Table—4.114 Records maintained by the Respondents

	CGL	SKHT	PLNR	TPL	TPT	Total	%
Monthly Progress Report (MPR)	4	4	6	5	4	23	100.0
Food Consolidating Rag (FCR)	–	4	–	5	–	9	39.1
Survey	4	–	–	–	4	8	34.8
C.L	4	–	–	5	–	9	39.1
I.G.A	4	–	6	–	–	10	43.5
I.M.K	4	–	–	5	–	9	39.1
GCP	4	–	–	5	–	9	39.1
Referral	4	–	6	–	4	14	60.9
Duty certificate register	–	–	–	5	–	5	21.7
Foodstock	–	4	6	5	4	19	82.6
Medicine stock	–	–	–	5	4	9	39.1
Bio-data Register	–	–	6	–	–	6	26.1
Mahila mandal Register	–	–	6	–	–	6	26.1
Immunization	–	4	–	–	–	4	17.4
Pre-natal and post-natal service register	–	4	6	–	4	10	43.5
Birth and deaths register	–	4	–	–	–	4	17.4
Grades register	–	4	–			4	17.4
Visitors register	–	4	–	–	–	4	17.4

problems in the implementation of the ICDS programme, among the rest, lack of proper own building is one of the problems for 26% of the respondents as it is very difficult to find a building with the meagre amount of rent given in the project. Seventeen per cent of the respondents told that, as they could not offer loans in time, they are facing problems from the IMK groups. Usually each supervisor is required to supervise and guide the work of 20 Anganwadi workers in rural project, but thirteen per cent of the respondents especially in Thamballapalle project were supervising nearly 40 AWCs, hence the increase in work load for the respondents. Rejection of SNF, Lack of community participation, Transportation of SNF bags etc were the other problems facing by the respondents.

Table—4.115 Problems encountered in Implementation of the Project

Problems	CGL	SKHT	PLNR	TPL	TPT	Total	%
Lack of proper building	–	2	–	3	–	5	21.7
Rejection of SNF due to worms	–	–	–	3	–	3	13.0
Delay in giving IMK loans	4	–	–	–	–	4	17.4
Excessive work load (40 centres)	–	–	–	3	–	3	13.0
Limited amount as rent	–	–	–	–	1	1	4.3
Lack of people's participation	–	–	3	–	–	3	13.0
Transportation of SNF	–	1	–	–	–	1	4.3
Nothing	–	1	3	2	3	9	39.1

Though they have some problems in the implementation of this programme it has met some of the needs of their village people and they also told that the programme has improved the health and nutritional status of the mothers and children because of the services like SNF distribution, Immunization, Growth monitoring. Health check-up, Health and Nutritional education and distribution of medicines etc.

In the present study all the AWCs were found to have clean indoor and outdoor space and availability of

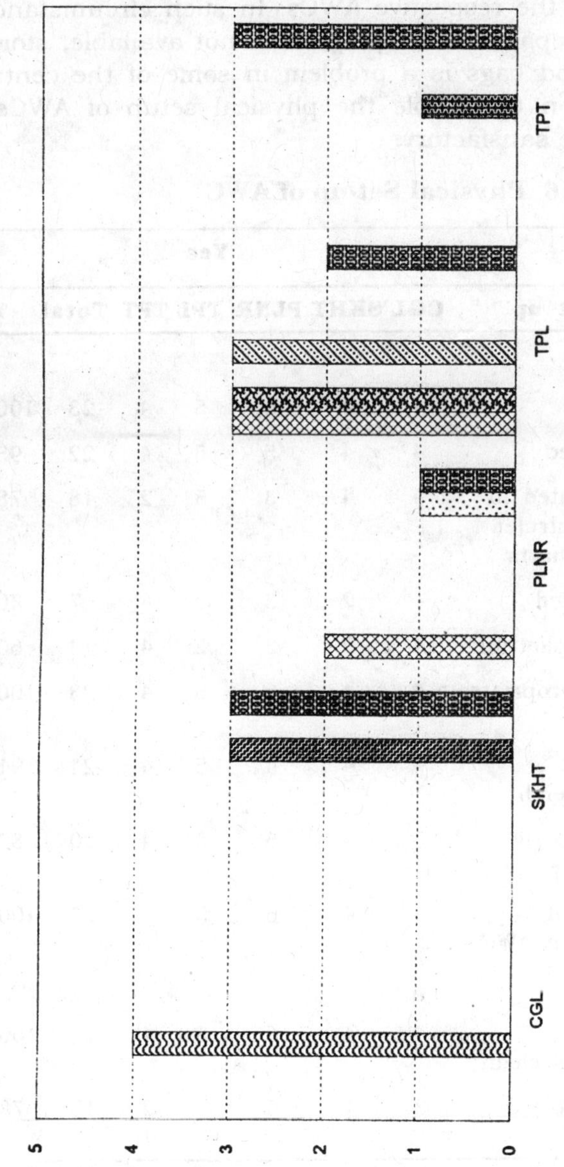

Fig. 4.24: Problems Encountered in Implementation of the Project

safe drinking water. The ration for distribution of SNF is supplied in bulk to AWCs at regular intervals. It is stocked at the respective AWCs. In such circumstances, wherever separate storage space is not available, storage of such food bags is a problem in some of the centres. However, on the whole the physical setup of AWCs is found to be satisfactory.

Table—4.116 Physical Set-up of AWC

	Yes						
Physical set up	**CGL**	**SKHT**	**PLNR**	**TPL**	**TPT**	**Total**	**%**
Indoor							
Clean	4	4	6	5	4	23	100.0
Well arranged	4	4	5	5	4	22	95.7
Children seated in rows/semi-circles	4	4	3	5	2	18	78.3
Display of charts							
Torn and faded	–	2	3	2	–	7	30.4
Fresh and colourful	4	2	2	2	4	14	60.9
Content appropriate for age	4	4	6	5	4	23	100.0
Displayed at children's height	4	4	4	5	4	21	91.3
Rations properly stored	3	4	5	3	4	20	87.0
Availability of clean water at AWC	4	4	6	5	4	23	100.0
Outdoor							
Immediate surroundings clean	4	4	6	5	4	23	100.0
Space available & used for play	3	4	5	4	2	18	78.3

(Contd...)

Physical set up	No						
	CGL	SKHT	PLNR	TPL	TPT	Total	%
Indoor							
Clean	–	–	–	–	–	–	–
Well arranged	–	–	1	–	–	1	4.3
Children seated in rows/semi-circles	–	–	3	–	2	5	21.7
Display of charts							
Torn and faded	4	2	3	3	4	16	69.6
Fresh and colourful	–	2	4	3	–	9	39.1
Content appropriate for age	–	–	–	–	–	–	–
Displayed at children's height	–	–	2	–	–	2	8.7
Rations properly stored	–	–	1	2	–	3	13.0
Availability of clean water at AWC	–	–	–	–	–	–	–
Out door							
Immediate surroundings clean	–	–	–	–	–	–	–
Space available & used for play	1	–	1	1	2	5	8.7

As per the data shown in Table 4.117, the respondents told that there is an improvement in the enrolment of beneficiaries every year except in Thamballapalle and Palamaneru projects, 20-25 children were attending pre-school during the visit of the supervisor. On the whole not less than 15 children were attending in all the centres and majority of them were staying for full duration of the school at Anganwadi centres.

Table—4.117 Number of Children Attending Pre-School During the Visit

Number of children	CGL	SKHT	PLNR	TPL	TPT	Total	%
15–20	–	2	4	4	–	10	43.5
20–25	4	2	2	1	4	13	56.5
Total	**4**	**4**	**6**	**5**	**4**	**23**	**100**

Performance of Pre-school Children

The findings of the performance of pre-school children indicates a fairly satisfactory trend. According to all the respondents majority of their pre-school children could identify the colours and different shapes. Except 3 respondents of CGL project, remaining told that. majority of their pre-school children could count, recite four or five rhymes and they also appeared to be very happy in attending the school.

Health and Nutrition

Nutritional intervention is a strategy to promote nutritional status of the target population and to combat malnutrition, reduce the problem of low birth weight babies and prevalence of nutritional deficiencies. In the present study findings revealed that AWWs enrolled all the mothers and children, who were at risk and the health staff also visits the AWC once in every month. To create better awareness on health and nutrition all the AWWs used to conduct meetings for women during the month. The general topics covered were foods to be taken during pregnancy, weaning foods, ORS preparation, cooking practices, nutritive foods like green leafy vegetables, ragi and need of immunization and family planning etc. According to all the respondents, the supplementary nutrition food is cooked and served under hygienic conditions.

Community Participation

Community participation in the context of child development is not a mere formality but a need for effective implementation of the programme. Hence, all the respondents had contact with the community representatives like sarpanch, primary school teacher, Mahilamandal members etc. According to the respondents except some AWWs, majority of the AWWs in their sectors were capable to mobilize the community support effectively and they also made required home visits.

Teaching Aids and Materials

The information pertaining to teaching aids and materials is presented in Table 4.118. According to the data more than three-fourths of the respondents told that the AWW uses teaching aids frequently while teaching and makes the children to play with play materials also. In their view the materials which were there in AWCs are in usable condition.

Table—4.118 Teaching Aids and Materials

Details	CGL	SKHT	PLNR	TPL	TPT	Total	%
AWW uses teaching aids frequently	4	3	6	2	4	19	82.6
Children are given play material frequently	4	2	6	1	4	17	73.9
New aids and play material were made	1	3	5	5	4	18	78.3
Materials maintained in usable condition	–	4	6	5	4	19	82.6

With regard to the suggestions given by the supervisors for effective functioing of the AWCs, the Table 4.119 shows the nature of suggestions.

Table—4.119 Suggestions Given by Supervisors

Suggestions	CGL	SKHT	PLNR	TPL	TPT	Total	%
AWW should be a local woman	–	2	1	–	–	3	13.0
Honorarium of AWW must be increased	–	1	–	–	–	1	4.3
Proper AWC building must be constructed	4	2	–	–	–	6	26.1
Minimum qualification of AWW should be 10th Standard	–	2	–	–	–	2	8.7
More medicines to be supplied to AWC	–	–	–	2	2	4	17.4
Publicity about AWCs is required	–	–	–	4	–	4	17.4
More playing materials must be given to AWC	4	–	–	–	–	4	17.4
Required equipment must be provided to AWC	–	–	1	–	–	1	4.3
New schemes must be introduced	–	–	1	–	–	1	4.3
Funds must be utilised in a proper way	–	–	1	–	–	1	4.3
Sincerity among the functionaries is important	–	–	1	–	–	1	4.3
No suggestions	–	–	2	1	2	5	21.7

Majority(78%) of the respondents have given suggestions for better implementation of the project. Of these own buildings must be constructed which is an

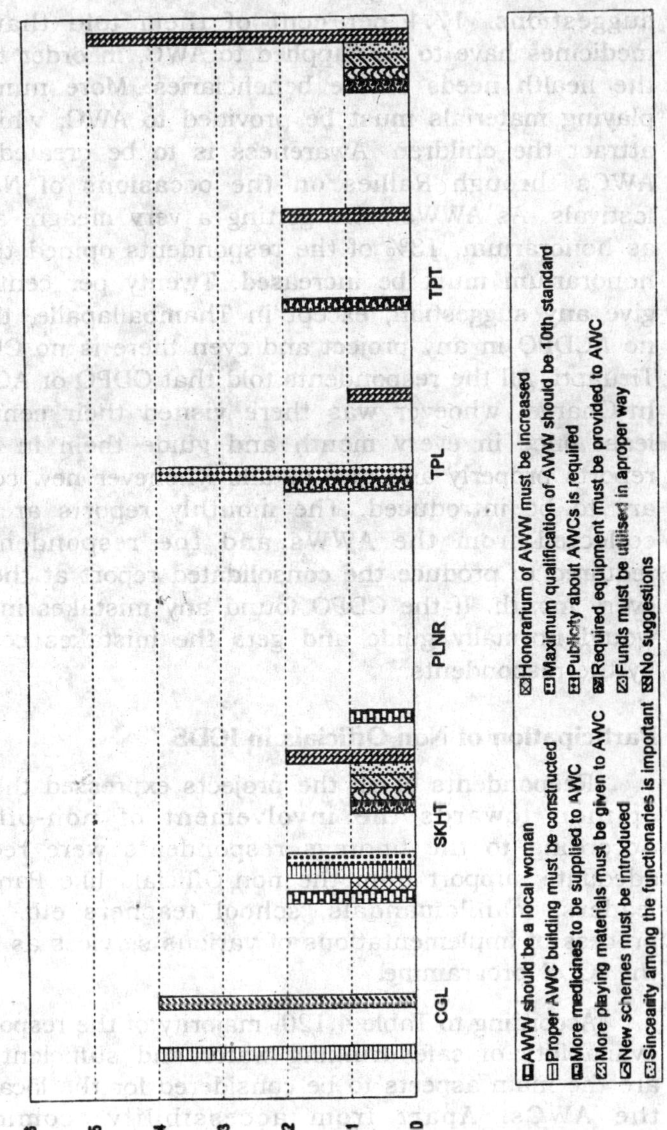

Fig. 4.25: Suggestions Given by Supervisors

essential requirement for the functioning of the centre and for conducting the programme is one of the suggestions. 17.4 per cent of them told that more medicines have to be supplied to AWC, in order to meet the health needs of the beneficiaries. More number of playing materials must be provided to AWC, which will attract the children. Awareness is to be created about AWCs through Rallies on the occasions of National festivals. As AWWs were getting a very meagre amount as honorarium, 13% of the respondents opined that the honorarium must be increased. Twenty per cent didn't give any suggestion, except in Thamballapalle, there is no ACDPO in any project and even there is no CDPO in Tiruapti. All the respondents told that CDPO or ACDPO / In-Charge, whoever was there visited their centres at least once in every month and guide them in writing reports properly and give details whenever new schemes are to be introduced. The monthly reports are to be collected from the AWWs and the respondents are required to produce the consolidated report at the office every month. If the CDPO found any mistakes in it she would normally guide and gets the mistakes corrected by the respondents.

Participation of Non-Officials in ICDS

Respondents of all the projects expressed the same opinion towards the involvement of non-officials. According to the findings respondents were receiving adequate support from the non-Officials like Panchayat leaders, mahilamandals, school teachers etc. in the process of implementations of various services as part of the ICDS programme.

According to Table 4.120, majority of the respondents availability of safe drinking water and sufficient space are the main aspects to be considered for the location of the AWCs. Apart from accessibility, community co-operation and economic conditions of the people in the area which are also to be taken in to consideration while locating AWCs.

Fig. 4.26: Criteria in Locating AWC

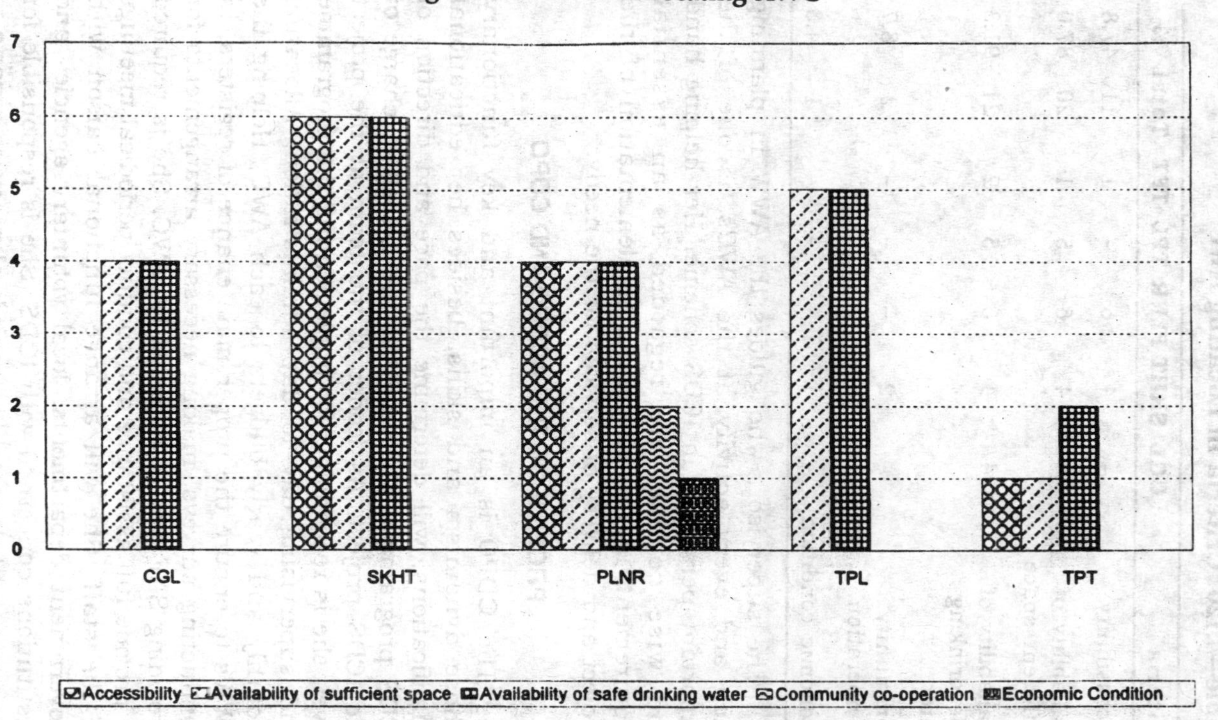

Table—4.120 Criteria in Locating AWC

Criteria	CGL	SKHT	PLNR	TPL	TPT	Total	%
Accessibility	–	4	6	–	1	11	47.8
Availability of sufficient space	4	4	6	5	1	20	87.0
Availability of safe drinking water	4	4	6	5	2	21	91.3
Community co-operation	–	2	–	–	–	2	8.7
Economic condition	–	1	–	–	–	1	4.3

The supervisor, who guides the AWW in planning each and every activity at the AWCs, is one of the important personnel in ICDS scheme. Her helping hand and wise counsel are regarded as an essential requirement in the successful implementation of the project and delivery of services for the needy.

PROFILE OF THE ACDPO AND CDPO

The CDPO is an important and key functionary whose dynamism and skills, besides her educational qualifications, will determine the pace and direction of ICDS programme. The CDPO is the overall in charge of the ICDS project. As leader of the team at the project level, she is responsible for implementing the programme and supervising day to day administration. Allocating monthly and yearly budgets to each AWC, Helping the AWWs to ensure the proper maintenance of registers, in conducting surveys, making necessary arrangements for providing SNF and equipments for AWC. She is required to provide full assistance and conduct periodical meetings of the staff. She will arrange functional liaison with Government departments, local voluntary agencies and institutions concerned with ICDS. She is responsible for preparing and despatching periodical progress reports to concerned higher officials. In addition she should make efforts to arrange own buildings of AWCs. Co-ordinate with urban development department, Rural water supply department, to install smokeless chullas, sanitary latrines and hand pumps. She should implement the new schemes meant for women and child development.

As there is no CDPO, the Medical officer is incharge of ICDS Project in Tirupati, only 4 CDPOs and one ACDPO of Thamballapalle project could be interviewed. All the respondents were between 40 to 60 years of age. All the respondents belonged to forward caste and Hindu by religion except one who is a Christian. Except one, all of them were having 2 children; 80% of them were living in nuclear family.

Regarding their educational qualifications, two have completed their SSC, two are graduates and the remaining one has completed Post-graduation. Three respondents owned neither land nor house, one is having own house on her husband's name and another owned 2.5 acres of land. The total emoluments of the respondents is Rs. 6000/- for four, more than seven thousand for the remaining, per month. Two-thirds of these respondents had 15-25 years of experience and the remaining had 25-35 years of experience in various Government departments, like women and child welfare, Revenue, Panchayat Raj etc. Except onc (ACDPO) who had been appointed three months ago all the respondents had 1 to 4 years of experience as CDPO. Three of the respondents were supervisors before they became CDPOs. Among the remaining, one was Executive Officer (EO) in Panchayat Raj department, another was ACDPO. All of them were selected as CDPO/ACDPO through promotion by the project officer or the commissioner of women development and child welfare. Only 3 respondents have attended the training programmes for about 40 days and 10 days of refresher coursc conducted by NIPCCD. In the view of 2 respondents, the training made them to re-call their responsibilities, duties etc as they had the previous experience. As the remaining were promoted from E.O

(Panchayat Raj) to CDPO, they expressed that they learned several things through such trainings.

Job Performance

All the respondents told that, though several government officials are involved in the implementation of ICDS project, the CDPO is the principal executive functionary. The specific nature of their work is that they should act as the co-ordinator of the ICDS at project level. An important responsibility is to supervise and guide the work of the entire project team, including supervisor and AWW. They also told that they are responsible in the implementation of various schemes, distribution of salary, checking of registers etc. According to them, offering Nutrition and health education to all women in the age group of 15-45 years, follow-up activities to children who suffer from frequent illness, cooking demonstrations and home visits etc., which will directly improve the health status of women and indirectly the social status of women and children. All the respondents accepted that the ICDS programme has improved the health and nutritional status of women and this is due to the proper utilization of the services.

As far as the respondents assessment towards the performance of AWCs in their concerned area, 3 expressed that they were satisfied with the performance of all the centres in their area. According to one respondent, 75% of centres were functioning satisfactorily and the remaining told that 50% of the centres were only working up to the mark. Illiteracy and poor economic conditions of the people, infrastructural limitations, finance, lack of peoples participation etc were the common impediments in the successful implementation of ICDS programme.

An attempt was made to collect the suggestions of the respondents to strengthen the programme. According to their views, AWW should be an efficient local woman and appointment of Grade I supervisors are also necessary for the successful implementation of the programme. Regarding the monthly reports, AWW is responsible to prepare monthly reports at the centre level. It is the responsibility of the supervisor to check and consolidate the Monthly Progress Reports (MPR) given by all the AWWs in their sector and produce them in the office of the CDPO. Finally the CDPO/ACDPO checks the MPRs comparing them with previous monthly reports, and the consolidated project report will be sent to project director at district level.

All the respondents opined that the officials of various departments like health, social welfare, women welfare and rural development, have specific roles to play in promoting co-operation and co-ordination in improving the nutritional and health status by providing immunization and medical aid and in improving the economic status by giving loans through self help groups etc. They also told that they had the effective co-ordination between various departments.

All of them told that participation of non-officials is also very essential requirement, especially their help is essential in mobilising the community, in providing accommodation to run the AWC, in the successful implementation of immunization etc. And none of them have experienced any problem with regard to the involvement of non-officials. As the supervisor can not supervise all the AWCs every day, the local leaders like panchyat president, ward members should be requested to look after the centres for effective implementation of various services.

5 Major Findings and Suggestions

The study was conducted in five ICDS projects of Chittoor district by covering 10 AWCs in each project. The study covers 500 beneficiaries of various services offered by the scheme along with 50 AWWs, 23 supervisors, an ACDPO and 4 CDPOs.

The enquiries revealed that half of the pre-school children were between 2 to 4 years. The study shows that 65% of mothers of pre-school children, 80% of pregnant women, 76% of lactating mothers were between 18-28 years. Majority of them were from backward caste category followed by forward castes, only one-fourth of them were from scheduled caste and scheduled tribe category. Seventy per cent of them had small families with one or two children. About 50% of beneficiaries of the three categories, mothers of pre-school children, pregnant women and lactating mothers were housewives and illiterates. All of them were satisfied with the immunization service, 34.4% of them have expressed their dissatisfaction towards health check-up and referral services. 100% of them told that they met AWW atleast once in a week either at home or at AWC. When asked their opinion on the overall functioning of AWC, all of them expressed their satisfaction except 3 beneficiaries. With regard to the immunization, more than 75% of them had correct knowledge regarding different types of vaccinations, except D.T. and 100% of the children got immunized either at AWC or PHC.

At the time of the study 47.3% of pregnant women were in 7-9 months of pregnancy followed by 40% who were in 5-7 months. Regarding their family income, large number of them ranged from Rs. 700-1100/- per month and expenditure on food was Rs. 300/-to 900/-. Though it is necessary to take additional foods during pregnancy, 30% of them could not add any additional foods to their normal meal due to their low economic status, and almost one-thirds of them avoided papaya, egg, mango, guava, black fruits etc due to ignorance about the nutritional value. Except 3 members, all the other were getting SNF daily but the amount they consumed was not even 90 grms. Monotonous taste, identical preparation every day, fear of stomach pain, indigestion etc., were the main complaints form the beneficiaries. Regarding lactating mothers, 63% of them extended their help to AWW in conducting meetings and at the time of vaccination etc.

To understand their level of awareness regarding mothers at risk, three types of beneficiaries were asked to specify the mothers at risk, 50 to 80% of them opined that women with anaemia and women who have had abortions and frequent deliveries were identified as conditions of risk. Regarding the place where their children were treated when they fell ill, 36.3% of them told that they went to private clinics followed by PHC and even some of them were going for folk medicine and appeasing of Gods, instead of going to hospitals as they have faith on such type of healing systems.

The findings with regard to AWWs, all of them were between 20 to 50 years of age and 50% of them from backward caste category. As educational qualifications are flexible for the appointment of AWW, only 34% had college education and having 3 to 15 years of experience as AWW. Only 7.8% of them were local women. Majority of them felt that giving immunization, conducting pre-school and distributing SNF, only as their responsibilities. Eighty per cent of AWCs were functioning in rented buildings by paying a rent of about Rs. 50-150/- month. About three-fourth of the centres were having neither toilet facilities nor separate store room to store things, but all the centres had safe drinking water facilities. It was found that most of the anganwadi workers were of the opinion that they have not been given proper teaching aids except charts and some toys. 7.2% of the AWWs have experienced community co-operation. It was noticed that 15 to 55 children were enrolled for pre-school but only 15 to 38 children were attending regularly in each centre. 60% of them have expressed that they were facing several problems in the implementation of the scheme and they all also told that in spite of the problems they faced the scheme solved several problems of the people of the villages where they were working.

With regard to supervisors 70% of them were between 30 to 40 years of age and majority of them completed their 10th class, 26% of them have completed their Post-graduation. Nearly 50% of them became supervisors through promotion and all of them were having 1 to 15 years of experience as supervisor. 70% of them expressed several problems in the implementation of this programme and have given suggestions to improve the programme. They pointed that every AWC should have proper building, teaching aids and playing materials as these are essential requirements for the successful implementation of the scheme.

All the CDPOs and ACDPOs of the present study were between 40 to 60 years of age and having 1 to 4 years of experience as CDPOs and with regard to their educational qualifications two have completed their SSC, 2 were graduates and the remaining was a Post-graduate. As far as the respondents assessment towards the performance of AWCs in their concerned area, 3 of them have expressed that they were satisfied with the performance of all the centres in their area, but the remaining told that only 50-75% of the centres were working up to the mark.

Impact of ICDS

1. ICDS programme has considerably improved its capacity to reach the children in the vulnerable age group.
2. There are very few studies on the evaluation of overall performance of the AWWs.
3. No uniformity in performance was observed for all components. For ex. some of them are found to be good in pre-school education and some are good in immunization.
4. ICDS has produced the desired impact on its beneficiaries and brought an improvement in some of the components. But there is a need to strengthen ICDS and to further enhance its potential in bringing about ultimate change in the life of the people.
5. The role of training, use of mass media and the contents of the programme need to be reviewed and analysed to make this component more effective.
6. ICDS functionaries felt that the job training received was too theoretical and did not equip them with enough skills to cope with the field situation.
7. A majority of ICDS functionaries were not able to perceive the importance of community participation.
8. The present system of monitoring of ICDS emphasizes the process of delivering services and does not highlight, the quality of services rendered.

The root cause of under development and decreased productivity is poor nutritious and health status for any individual. Therefore it is imperative that the ICDS which was initiated with prime purpose of improving the nutritional health status of children and women should be continued. However the feedback indicates that there are several areas in the functioning of ICDS which needs to be strengthened. Such efforts would contribute significantly to provide health for all by 2000 A.D.

Efforts to Strengthen ICDS

1. ICDS coverage has to improve in terms of reaching the vulnerable children and women. This is possible through motivating AWWs to enrol all subjects who deserve these supportive services.
2. All components of ICDS services should be given equal attention rather than concentrating only on providing supplementary food immunization and pre-school education.
3. The quality of performance of the Anganwadi worker must be improved by providing her with training and establishing her credibility in the community.
4. The training components should be a reflection of the field requirements rather than theory.
5. ICDS functionaries at all levels should be convinced of the importance of community participation.
6. A continuous monitoring of ICDS services delivery system is required to improve the quality of services provided through the programme.

Suggestions

Specific suggestions offered to improve the programme in the area where the study was conducted are as follows:

Through the study it has been found that the scheme is being implemented satisfactorily. Still the following suggestions can be taken into consideration for further improvement and for the effective implementation of the scheme.

- As it is really difficult to get a building with a rent of Rs. about 150/- per month in urban areas with all essential requirements, funds allocation towards rent should be increased.
- Proper accommodation for AWC is a necessary pre-requisite for the successful implementation of the programme. In some of the centres often activities are organised in the open area or under a tree. But during rainy season this arrangement is not possible, more over, lack of proper room also created problem for safe keeping of equipment, utensil, teaching aids etc. Hence it is recommended that every AWC should have a proper building.
- Periodical supervision and effective monitoring of the work of each and every employee by their higher official is needed which would improve the responsibility of each functionary and would pave way for better implementation of the programme. Efforts should be made to enhance professional growth of AWWs by giving assistance in carrying out the administrative tasks to reduce their work load. This will enable them to spend more time on pre-school education activities and to fulfill the major objectives of the scheme.
- Improvement in service conditions of AWWs like frequent in service training, incentives for better work may help in achieving better results.
- Honorarium of AWW should be increased to a reasonable level by keeping in mind the nature and quantum of work performed by them, along

with the level of inflation. So that they will have job satisfaction and would be able to concentrate on work which may help in achieving better results.

- AWW could be taken to various institutions which are located locally and in nearby areas to obtain knowledge regarding disabled children, methods of rehabilitation and other welfare activities.
- Concerted efforts are required on the part of medical and health department to fulfill the desired goal of Health for all by 2000.
- As part of immunization programme efforts should be made to concentrate on Booster doses of vaccines and TT which is to be given to pregnant women.
- The supply of essential medicines should be ensured along with adequate support and an inbuilt referral system.
- As immunization and health check-ups are being implemented with the co-ordination of Health Department, the efforts of AWW are not being appreciated by the community.
- The health and nutrition education component needs to be strengthened as the present education imparted by AWW has a limited impact on the health of children.
- More emphasis should be laid to utilise nearby outdoor space for organising programmes for children.
- Supply of teaching aids and toys for play can be increased in number which are an essential requirements to attract the children to AWCs.
- Regular contacts among the staff can be maintained to review and monitor the functioning of the centres.

- The level of community participation is rather low, than expected. An important aspect in ICDS is the provision of accommodation to run AWC. Community co-operation can be ensured by AWW not only in this aspect but their co-operation should be sought to implement other services effectively.
- Quality of weaning food can be taken into consideration and efforts should made to improve it so that it is readily accepted, instead of giving same food every day, various recipes should be evolved based on low cost local food items.
- Wide publicity about the scheme should be given through personal contacts and mass media to create awareness among the community.

Bibliography

1. Arun Chopdar,. *Integrated Child Development Services—Its Activities in Orissa*. Ind. J. Pediatr., 46: 53, 1979.

2. Asha Srivastava, Kishi Agarwal and Deeksha Kapoor. *"Parental Participation with Special Reference to Their Satisfaction and Functioning of Anganwadi Centres"*. Research Abstracts on Integrated Child Development Services. NIPCCD, New Delhi, 1978.

3. Baradha, G. and Jyothimani, P. *"Impact of ICDS Social Components on Children and Mothers"*, Res. High, JADU. Vol. 3 (4) pp.142-148, 1994.

4. Basu R.N, Deeepak Phalgune, Maya Natu. *Review of Assessment of Immunization in ICDS*. Paper presented at the National Conference on Research on ICDS, Publ. NIPCCD, 1986.

5. Chowdary, N.D. *"Anganwadi Workers in a Tribal Belt"*, Social Welfare, Vol. XXXIV (7). pp.14-15, 1987.

6. Deepak Phalgune, Maya Natu and Sanjay Mehendale. *Beneficiary Women's Views on Some Aspects of ICDS*. Abstract of Research Papers, 1986.

7. Desai, A.B. *"Weight for Height, a Better Parameter for Identifying Severe Malnutrition than Weight for Age"*. B.J. Medical College, Ahmedabad. Abstracts of research papers. IX Annual convention of ICDS. Central Technical Committee on Health and Nutrition, AIIMS, 1985.

8. Geetha, M. *"Utilization of Primary Health Services in Two ICDS Project Areas*, M.Sc Thesis, Dept. of Home Science, S.V. University, Tirupati, 1989.

9. Gopalan, C. Nutrition Foundation of India, *"ICDS A Study of Some Aspects of the System"*, Scientific Report, 1988.

10. Govt. of India . *"Manual on Integrated Management Information System for ICDS"* Ministry of Human Resource Development. Dept. of Women's Welfare, New Delhi, 1986.

11. Jaya, S and Siva Jyothi Kondraju. *"Creating Awareness Among Mothers of AW Children on Health Practices"* Res. High. JADU, Vol. 6(4). pp.190-193, 1996.

12. Juliana Sharma and Sithalakshmi, S. *"Role Performance of Anganwadi Workers (AWWs) Trained in Different Institutions"*, Res. High. JADU, 7, pp.76-79, 1997.

13. Swarupa . K. *"Nutritional Status and Awarness of the Pregnant Women in an Urban ICDS Project"*. M.Sc thesis, Dept. of Home Science, S.V. University, Tirupati, 1986.

14. Komala. *"Evaluation of Nutrition Knowledge of AWWs of Tirupati ICDS Project*. M. Phil Thesis, S.V. University, Tirupati, 1992.

15. Krishnamurthy, K.G and Nadkarni. *Integrated Child Development Services: An Assessment*. UNICEF, (1983).

16. Lal, S and Joshi, V.S. *Mid Course Assessment of Impact* of ICDS *Programme on Nutritional Status in Pre-school Children in Kathura Block (Haryana)*. Ind. J. Prev. and Sco. med, 1977.

17. Lata Narayanan. *Monitoring and Evaluation of Social Component of Integrated Child Development Services Programme*. Tata Institute of Social Sciences, Bombay, 1991.

18. Mandowara, S.L. *Monitoring of Children Severe Grade Protein Energy Malnutrition in ICDS Block*, Chhoti Sadri, Rajasthan, 1977.

19. Maria Kamalam and Jaya, N. *"Training the Anganwadi Workers in Timely Detection of Disabilities in Children"*, Res. High, JADU, Vol.3(4), pp.221-225, 1993.

20. Mehta, N.R, *et al.,. Decline in ICDS Activities due to Absence of Senior Surpervisory Staff in a Tribal ICDS Block in Valod* in Surat district, Surat (Gujarat), Medical College, Surat, Dept. of Preventive and Social Medicine, 1985.

21. Nancy Nagoori. Unpublished M.Sc. Thesis on *"Knowledge of Anganwadi Workers in Identification of Various Disabilities Among Pre-school Children in Tirupati"*. Dept. of Human Development and Family Studies, S.P.M.V.V, Tirupati, 1997.

22. NIPCCD. *National Evaluation of Integrated Child Development Services,* New Delhi, 1997.

23. NIPCCD. *"Monitoring and Evaluation of Social Components in ICDS"*, Guidelines for involvement of Technical Institutions, New Delhi, 1984.

24. NIPCCD. *Assigning the Responsibility of Screening and Growth Monitoring of Child in ICDS,* 1984.

25. NIPCCD. *Prevention and Early Detection of Childhood Disability—Role of Anganwadi Worker,* New Delhi, 1984.

26. Prabhavathamma, P. *"Community Participation in ICDS"* unpublished M.Sc thesis, Dept. of Home Science, S.V. University, Tirupati, 1988.

27. Parvathi Rao, K. *"Socio-cultural Factors and Malnutrition in Telengana Region of A.P"*, Proc. Nutr. Soc. India 6, 1968.

28. Parvathi Rao. K. PEO, Planning Commission, Govt. of India, *Evaluation Report of the Integrated Child Development Services Projects,* 1976-1978. New Delhi, 1982.

29. Pramila, H., V. Kittu and P. Gopala Krishna. *"Health Education for Success of ICDS Programme"*. ICDS. Res. abs., published by NIPCCD, New Delhi, 1986.

30. Rajagopal, J. *"Impact of ICDS on Nutrition and Health"* Res. abs, ICDS Central Cell, All India Institute of Medical Sciences, New Delhi, 1985.

31. Rajani & Punam Cahri. *"Review of Research on Supplementary Nutrition in ICDS"* NIPCCD, New Delhi, 1992.

32. Rajesh Dahiya and Sharma, R.K. *"Anganwadi Workers: What are their Constraints"*? Social Welfare, Vol.XXXVII (8) pp.35. 1990.

33. Ray, C.N. *"Implementation of Integrated Community Development Service in Eastern Uttar Pradesh"*, Social Change. Sep. Vol.20, No.3, 1990.

34. Renuka Khosla and Meena Katari. *"Meetings with Parents" Journal of Pre-school Education in ICDS—An Impact Study—A Report,* 184, 1986.

35. Rita Punhani, Rachna Mahajan. *"Research on Integrated Child Development Service: An Overview"*, Vol. 1, 1975-85. NIPCCD, New Delhi, 1989.

36. Santhana Krishna, B.R and Madhusudhan, B. *Knowledge, Attitude Practices of Young Mothers in ICDS Project (Urban slums) to "GOBIFF"*. Abstracts of Research papers, IX Annual convention of ICDS. Central Technical Committee on Health and Nutrition, AIIMS, 1985.

37. Sharma, Adar. *Monitoring Social Components of Integrated Child Development Services: A Pilot Project*, New Delhi, NIPCCD, 1987.

38. Sunderlal and Vasudeva, Y.L. *"Better Primary Health Care Services Utilisation Through ICDS in Haryana"*. Ind. J. Paediat, 47: 293, 1980.

39. Swarnalatha Devi. *"Nutritional Status of Pregnant Women of Urban Slums Covered by the ICDS Project"* Unpublished M.Sc thesis, Dept. of Home Science, S.V. University, Tirupati, 1986.

40. Tondon, B.N. et al. *Integrated Child Development Services in India. Objectives, Organisation and Baseline Survey of the Project Population.* Ind. J. Med. Res. 73, 1981.

41. Tondon, B.N., Ramachandran, K and Bhatnagar, S. *Integrated Child Development Services in India, Evaluation of the Delivery of Nutrition and the Effect of the Nutritional Status of the Children*, 1981.

42. Vasudeva, Y.L. *"Knowledge, Attitudes and Practices in Relation to Nutrition of Mothers in an ICDS Block"*, Res. abs. ICDS Central Cell, AIIMS., New Delhi, 1983.

43. Visweswara Rao and Gopalan, C. *"Nutrition and Family Size"* of Nut. and Dietetics, 6, 1969.

Annexure—I

Abbreviations

ACDPO	-	Assistant Child Development Project Officer
ANM	-	Auxilliary Nurse Midwife
APER	-	Andhra Pradesh Economic Restructuring Project
APPSC	-	Andhra Pradesh Public Service Commission
ASCI	-	Administrative Staff College of India
AWC	-	Anganwadi Center
AWW	-	Anganwadi Worker
BCG	-	Bacillus Calmette Guerin
BP	-	Blood Pressure
CARE	-	Co-operative American Relief Everywhere
CDPO	-	Child Development Project Officer
CGL	-	Chinnagottigallu
CL	-	Casual Leave
CTC	-	Central Technical Committee
DPT	-	Diphtheria Pertussis Tetanus
DT	-	Diptheria Tetanus
DWCD	-	Department of Women and Child Development
DWCRA	-	Development of Women and Children in Rural Areas
FLAW	-	Functional Literacy for Adult Women
GCP	-	Girl Child Protection
GLV	-	Green Leafy Vegetables

H&N	-	Health and Nutrition
ICDS	-	Integrated Child Development Services
IMK	-	Indira Mahila Kosh
IMR	-	Infant Mortality Rate
LHV	-	Lady Health Visitor
MCH	-	Maternal and Child Health
MPR	-	Monthly Progress Report
NAEP	-	National Adult Education Programme
NGO	-	Non-governmental Organization
NHE	-	Nutrition and Health Education
NIN	-	National Institute of Nutrition
NIPCCD	-	National Institute of Public Corporation and Child Development
NORAD	-	Norway Agency for Development
ORS	-	Oral Rehydration Solution
PEM	-	Protein Energy Malnutrition
PHC	-	Primary Health Centre
PLNR	-	Palamaneru
RASS	-	Rayalaseema Seva Samithi
RTE	-	Ready to Eat
SC	-	Scheduled Caste
SKHT	-	Srikalahasthi
SNF	-	Supplementary Nutrition Food
ST	-	Scheduled Tribe
TPL	-	Thamballapalle
TPT	-	Tirupati
TT	-	Tetanus Toxoid
UNICEF	-	United Nations Children's Emergency Fund
WFP	-	World Food Programme

Index